I SAW

GOD'S HAND

IN PAPUA NEW GUINEA!

Jeffery Bishop

TEACH Services, Inc.
P U B L I S H I N G
www.TEACHServices.com • (800) 367-1844

Copyright © 2023 Jeffery Bishop
Copyright © 2023 TEACH Services, Inc.
ISBN-13: 978-1-4796-1559-9 (Paperback)
ISBN-13: 978-1-4796-1560-5 (ePub)
Library of Congress Control Number: 2022918778

The website reference in this book has been shortened using a URL shortener and redirect service called 1ref.us, which TEACH Services manages. If you find that a reference no longer works, please contact us and let us know which one is not working so that we can correct it. TEACH Services is not responsible for the accuracy or permanency of any links.

Published by

TEACH Services, Inc.
PUBLISHING
www.TEACHServices.com • (800) 367-1844

TABLE OF CONTENTS

Our family who started the Gogodala Mission Project: Jeff, Stacy, Rachel, and Bobbi

CHAPTER 1

DECISION TO BECOME MISSIONARIES

Our daughter Stacy was very excited one day; she had just received notice that she had been accepted as a Pathfinder for the next teen mission trip to the Dominican Republic. When she returned, after two weeks of helping doctors perform surgeries, she told us that she wanted to return someday as a missionary doctor.

One year later, my wife, Bobbi, had some medical issues, and her doctors had found that she had a tumor that was at least the size of a grapefruit. She and I suspected that the diagnosis might turn out to be cancer. Unfortunately, they could not tell yet whether the tumor was cancerous. It would be several weeks before we would know, after surgery was performed.

The tumor turned out to be just fibrous. Because of the surgery, however, she faced a six-week recovery period during which she would not be allowed to lift more than a fork or a spoon. All she was allowed to do was sit all day on a couch or recliner. She decided to take advantage of the time off work, and use that six-week period of recovery to renew her walk with the Lord.

For some reason, during her time in prayer and Bible study, she developed a strong feeling that our family should go to serve as missionaries overseas. Her major concern, however, was that she did not want to be separated from Stacy, our elder daughter, who was just about to enter the ninth grade. Then one night, while Bobbi was on her knees, she was arguing with the Lord about having to leave Stacy here in America to attend a boarding academy here while the rest of us were to travel to what could turn out to be a remote part of the world.

While she was literally arguing with God about leaving Stacy behind, she heard someone say, "I asked Abraham to give up his son and he didn't question me."

Because what she had heard was a physical voice, it was obvious that it had to be Jesus Christ Himself who had spoken audibly to her about our family becoming missionaries in a different part of the world. Because Jesus Christ Himself had literally spoken to her, she was convinced that our family needed to become missionaries. When she told me what happened, she asked if I would be willing to become a missionary.

My response to her was an emphatic *no.* I had just spent four years getting my teaching degree through the adult degree program at Southwestern Adventist University, and was in my second year of teaching at Grand Rapids Junior Academy, a job I loved. I had no intention of leaving teaching to go work as a missionary. I actually felt that my mission project was teaching the kids of our church at our school. But when Bobbi asked if she could send for a missionary application, I did not argue. However, when the application arrived, I simply never got around to filling it out.

Several months later, my brother Tim called me with a request. A missionary named Max Church, who had served as a General Conference Missionary in a French-speaking part of Africa, had recently retired. When he arrived back in America, he moved to Berrien Springs, Michigan, and started a private mission project in Haiti because French is spoken there, also.

I had no intention of leaving teaching to go work as a missionary.

He went to Tim's church in Benton Harbor, Michigan, where he spoke about his Haiti project and asked for donations. Because my brother had just become a nurse, and Max talked about his two medical clinics in Haiti, Tim decided he wanted to join Max's project.

Max told Tim that he needed to spend two weeks living there on another project to decide if that would work, so he asked him to help build a church with three other men. My brother agreed and traveled to Haiti, but because of bad weather, the job could not be completed. A short time later, Max found himself looking for someone to go back to Haiti and build the roof, to complete the church building.

Tim thought that since I had already finished building our own house, I would be able to finish the church; so he asked whether I would travel to Haiti and do that. My reply to my brother was another emphatic *no*. For several weeks after that, Bobbi continued to try to convince me to go to Haiti, but without success. I even told my brother a second time that I could not do that. Then one day, while having worship, my wife decided to ask the Lord to be the one to convince me to become a missionary.

A few weeks later, Tim called me a third time, again asking me whether I would consider going to Haiti to finish the church. At that time, I was in the middle of building a spec house in Grand Rapids, and I thought that my wife would not agree that I should go abroad with the project only half finished. I decided to let her say no, too, so my brother would stop asking me.

I put the phone up on my chest to muffle my voice and said to Bobbi, "It's my brother Tim again; he still wants me to go to Haiti and finish that church. What do you think I should tell him?" I was shocked when she said, "I think you could do that." I didn't know that my brother Tim and my wife had been collaborating behind the scenes, and that she had been encouraging Tim not to give up on asking me to go to Haiti.

Finally, I capitulated and told my brother that yes, I would go to Haiti. A few weeks later, my brother's daughter Korinn was attending her eighth-grade graduation service in Berrien Springs, Michigan. After the ceremony ended, they said they were going to let us have a potluck dinner. But it wasn't happening yet, so not wanting to waste time, my brother asked if I would like to drive over to the missionary's home to meet him. He was only about two miles from the school. I told him, "Yes, I would like to."

When we arrived, the overhead garage door was open, so we walked in up to his screen door, and saw that he was on his phone in his kitchen. Because he saw us coming, he motioned my brother and me to come on into his house. When we opened his door and walked in, I heard him say to the man on the phone, "Guess who just walked in—it's Tim, who was with you in Haiti. Do you want to talk to him, too?"

The guy said yes, so Max gave Tim the phone to talk to his friend before Tim could even introduce me to Max. As Max introduced himself to me, while shaking my hand, the first words out of his mouth were, "What I really need is someone to take over my entire organization in Haiti." A trip to put a roof on a church that my brother had started, was immediately transformed into a request for me to take over an orphanage, two medical clinics, and an elementary school in Haiti that Max Church had created.

All of a sudden, my wife's prayer request was answered. I was interested in mission service, especially because one of the projects was an elementary school. The problem, however, was that it was a self-supporting ministry, so I would need to raise funds. When I arrived back at the school and met with my wife, I told her, yes, I will become a missionary. I then told her that the Haiti mission was a self-supporting project, and she was then the one who answered with an emphatic *no!* What she had in mind was going with the General Conference, with insurance, a base salary, and a pension.

After she told me she would not serve as a self-supporting missionary, I talked to Max Church to tell him that we did not know how to raise money for a mission project so we probably would not be able to go to Haiti. Then Max mentioned something about an organization called Adventist Frontier Missions (AFM) right there in Berrien Springs. He told me that they sent missionaries all over the world. He suggested that we take a visit to AFM to see if we could learn how their missionaries raised funds.

Eventually, my wife agreed to visit AFM with me to learn if this self-supporting-missionary idea might work. Upon arriving at AFM, the person in charge of recruiting was not in the office, so his assistant, Vicki Wiley, took us into the conference room and shared AMF's philosophy. As we left AFM's office that day, we looked at each other and both of us felt that AFM was where we needed to be. When we arrived back home in Grand Rapids, we told our daughters, Stacy and Rachel, who were fourteen and ten years old, to watch the AFM videos and read the AFM magazines Vicki had given us. I told them that we would not talk about becoming missionaries for two weeks, and that after they watched the videos and read the magazines, we would decide what we should do.

When the two weeks were over, the four of us sat in a circle. I asked Rachel if she wanted our family to become missionaries with AFM and she said, "Yes, I do." I then asked Stacy if she wanted our family to become missionaries with AFM and she said, "Yes, I do, too." I knew Bobbi wanted to, but I asked her anyway, and she said yes! Then I said yes, too! If either of my daughters had said no, I would not have agreed anymore to become a missionary. That is why it is our two daughters, Stacy and Rachel, who created the Gogodala mission project.

CHAPTER 2

WHERE TO SERVE AS MISSIONARIES

$68,000.00. That is how much we needed to raise to start a mission project with AFM. Because I was worried about how I could raise almost seventy thousand dollars as a launching goal was why I wondered if I should decide to pursue my friend's suggestion that had happened.

One morning, I parked our car on a side street as we prepared to make a visit to AFM's office to sign up to become missionaries. Just as we stepped out of the car, another vehicle pulled up and parked right next to my car. The persons in that car were Johnny Cantor and his wife. I had known Johnny for thirty years. Johnny had been attending Andrews University to become a teacher and was working for my dad's pool business while attending the University.

Not only had Johnny worked for my dad, but his older two brothers and his younger sister had, too. Their family had moved from Canada to Berrien Springs to attend Andrews

University. Our family would travel with them to Canada to go fishing on lakes and rivers. When I was still in elementary school, Johnny married one of Danny Shelton's cousins. Danny is the founder of 3 Angels Broadcasting Network (3ABN).

After Johnny became a teacher, he continued to build pools during the summer. Then one year, when I was running our new warehouse out in Tyler, Texas, Johnny went there to build pools for me, too. When Johnny got out of his car and saw me, he said, "Jeff, is that you?" He was surprised to see me, so he asked me what had brought me back to Berrien Springs. When I told him that we were there to sign up with AFM to serve as missionaries, he asked me if I would have an interest in going to Russia to serve.

He asked me that because he had just come back from supervising the construction of 3ABN's new facility in Russia. Because he was a contractor, Danny Shelton had asked him if he would be in charge of building his new 3ABN department there. He told me that he had just finished the new facility and were now looking for someone to manage it, and he thought I was the one for the job. So he asked if I would be willing to move to Russia and run 3ABN's new facility.

I answered, "Yes, I could do that." He told me that he was going to tell Danny that I was the one they should send to Russia. I couldn't prove that I was going to be hired by Danny Shelton to do that, but if my lifelong friend Johnny was recommending me, then I expected it might actually happen.

To have to raise $68,000.00 plus $4,000.00 per month pledged support sounded a lot more complicated for me than simply pursuing a position that my friend Johnny had recommended for me. I decided not to pursue actively the 3ABN position because I wanted to let God make the decision for us, but I still signed on with AFM. During the four months I was submitting with AFM, no one from 3ABN ever called me.

Then one day, we again made a visit to the AFM office. This time it was to meet with the board for the final approval process for us to serve as an AFM missionary family. At the board meeting, the last question I was asked was, "Where do you want to serve as a missionary?" I had already discussed two projects with them. One was in the Philippines, and the other was in Papua New Guinea (PNG).

I actually preferred the Philippines because when I was serving as Pathfinder director in Tyler, Texas, my assistant was Filipino. But as I was ready to say, "the Philippines," for some reason, I said just, "You know what is needed, so you decide." After the board made their decision, our family was voted to start the Gogodala project in PNG.

When the meeting was over, we left the office and walked back to the same place where we had parked our car on our first visit. As Bobbi and I were walking down the same side-walk where I had met Johnny several months before, Johnny actually pulled up and got out of his car. Both of us were surprised to see each other again, in the exact same spot where we had met months earlier. Again Johnny asked me what had brought me back to Berrien Springs.

I responded, "We have just been accepted to start the Gogodala mission project in PNG with AFM. Immediately Johnny remembered asking if I would serve 3ABN in Russia and he said, "Jeff, I am so sorry; I completely forgot to tell Danny Shelton that you should be the manager." It was apparently God's plan that the Gogodala project in PNG should be our new home, and not Russia or the Philippines.

When we were approved to serve on the Gogodala project, we decided to sell our house. We hired a real estate agent, and she arrived on a Wednesday to work out a plan. When she told us the amount we should ask for, we told her that we needed to have our house sold within thirty days so we could start being taught by AFM how to become missionaries and go to live with Bobbi's mother while we were raising funds. She said she was not positive that the plan would be possible, but then recommended that we hold an open house on the following Sunday. Then, on Sunday afternoon, we were informed that our house was sold.

As we were then planning the move out of our house and into Bobbi's mother's basement while we raised funds, I advertised my table saw for sale. A young man called and said he would like to come see it. As I met him at our door, he made a comment that he heard that we were going to be missionaries.

I told him that it was true, and that we were going to work in PNG with the Gogodala people in the Western Province. He then told me something amazing. He told me that he, too, was a missionary in PNG. I became confused as to why someone who was living as a missionary in PNG would buy a table saw from me in America.

It was apparently God's plan that the Gogodala project in PNG should be our new home, and not Russia or the Philippines.

He explained that he served as a missionary near an aviation company in Goroka—he was an aircraft maintenance technician—and that they needed equipment to build a house for themselves. What was most amazing is that when we arrived in PNG and I flew one time to Goroka where Adventist Aviation was located, I realized that the company he worked for was right next to Adventist Aviation's department. I went over to meet him and thank him for purchasing my table saw.

CHAPTER 3

FUNDRAISING

As the process of fundraising began, we traveled from church to church, even as far as Washington State. We appeared on 3ABN to promote the Gogodala project as we raised our funds. It was during that time that Bobbi's employers told her that they wanted to do something to help us raise money for our mission project. One day we had a meeting with the two owners of that business and their wives, to discuss a plan.

Several ideas were discussed but, in the end, they settled on a fundraising dinner, complete with live entertainment from the Grand Ledge Quartet. I was still teaching geometry at Grand Rapids Junior Academy, so I gave my students an assignment. On graph paper, they were to arrange the gym with tables so that it would seat the most people possible. The total turned out to be 300 seats. It was in the gym at the Grand Rapids Junior Academy that we were going to have our fundraising dinner.

As the plans were laid, they decided to contact a caterer for the meal and charge each attendee $10.00, twice what the meal would cost, which would help us raise $1,500.00 that night if 300 people did arrive. That, however, just didn't seem like enough money to Bobbi's employers, so they offered to pay the caterer so our mission project could keep all $3,000.00 that might be raised if we could fill the gym.

Then my grandfather Albert Schilstra made a suggestion. He offered to donate up to $10,000.00 in matching funds for every dollar raised that night by the attendees. That then made the potential for raising funds to $3,000 for the fundraising dinner, plus what was donated by the attendees. On the night of the dinner, every one of the 300 seats in the gym was filled. As the people finished their meal and the music concluded, one of Bobbi's bosses stood up on the gym's stage because he wanted to make a joke. "As you all know," he said, "We are here tonight to get rid of the Bishops."

He announced the $10,000 matching pledge that had been proposed by my grandfather. Next, he said, "And tonight we are going to start that off with a $5,000.00 donation." That night, an additional $5,000.00 was raised from the congregation, making a total fundraising that night close to $23,000.00. The funds raised that night at the benefit dinner finished off our goal to raise $68,000.00. We were then able to be on our way to PNG.

CHAPTER 4

OUR NEW HOME

O ur family left America during the first week of July in 1997. We arrived at Port Moresby, the capital of PNG. We were allowed to stay at the Pacific Adventist University until we could fly to the Gogodala project in Western Province.

In PNG, all of the land belongs to the people. When you go to a village or a small town, some person owns every house and field. The government does not own any land unless they buy it from the local people for a school or hospital. For this reason, if a group of people do not want you to move into their village, there is no way you can move there. For thirty-one years, that was how the Gogodala people kept missionaries from coming to Balimo, after the ones who had created the Evangelical Church of Papua New Guinea (ECP) in 1966.

In one incident, a Seventh-day Adventist pastor had arrived among the Gogodala people to start a mission project. But the local Gogodala people took all of his EGW books and Bibles and threw them into the river, and then physically pushed him into an airplane to force him to leave.

This was the exact part of PNG that my family had been asked to move to, the Gogodala district in Western Province. The 600-mile-long Fly River flows through the province; its mouth is twenty-five miles wide. If an individual needs to travel from their part of the province to the Fly River, it is still five miles wide at the narrower point near our village.

Because the Fly River starts in the mountains of Western Province and flows to the southern part, the province is divided into three districts—the North Fly, Middle Fly, and South Fly. Balimo was the government center for the Middle Fly district, which is where the Gogodala mission project was expected to be started.

Australia governed PNG from 1906 to 1975. PNG gained its independence on September 16, 1975. In 1997, when we moved to Balimo, there had not been one single new modern home, office building, or even one nail driven in any building since September 16, 1975. All building and maintenance stopped on the day PNG gained its independence.

That is, until Roy Biyama started his businesses in Balimo. Roy was born in Balimo village, and as a young man he started selling popsicles on the streets. Roy had learned about freezer pops, and because his grandmother had a freezer in her house, he began using it to create popsicles for the people in his community. The average weather there was almost always 100 degrees, so popsicles were great to have. In selling those frozen treats, Roy began to make some money. He eventually was able to buy sugar, rice, beans, and canned fish to sell in Balimo.

Eventually, Roy decided to start a market store. By 1997, he and one other man owned the only two market stores in

Balimo. Roy soon became very rich. Eventually, he had made over ten thousand extra kina in his business. In PNG, the kina is the unit of currency, like the dollar in the United States America. To understand how rich Roy actually was, it helps to know that the average individual in Gogodala would make only about twenty-seven kina per year by selling coconuts and sago in the marketplace, to government workers. No one in the village could even afford to buy food. But government workers, including nurses, teachers, police officers, and members of the Middle Fly District, made at least sixty kina *per week*.

One day, Roy asked the company in Port Moresby, the capital of PNG, that supplied his store's goods, what he should do with his extra money. They told him that the government rented houses for all of its employees, and that if he wanted to make a lot of money, he should build modern houses to rent to the government in Balimo.

At that time, all of the government officers in Balimo were living in their own bush style houses. The government headquarters for the Middle Fly district had never been able to rent a house for an employee because not one house had been built among the Gogodala people since they had become an independent country in 1975. So Roy began to build four new houses to rent to the government. About six months later, he had the houses almost built. That's when the story gets interesting.

You see, Roy's brother, Silva, who lived in Port Moresby, was a Seventh-day Adventist. Roy would travel to Port Moresby to order supplies and to put his money in the bank because there was no bank in Balimo. When Roy would travel to Port Moresby, he would see Silva, who would talk to him about the Sabbath. On the second Sabbath in June of 1997, Roy's brother finally convinced Roy that he needed to close his store on the

Sabbath. On the third Sabbath that June, Roy finally started closing his store.

On the second day after we arrived in PNG, someone knocked on the door of the apartment at Pacific Adventist University, where we were staying. His name was Dale Goodson. He was already serving as a missionary in PNG with the Dowa people. He arrived to tell me that he would like to fly with me to Balimo to discuss the start of the Gogodala mission project. He had actually flown there a year earlier to verify for AFM that it was where they needed a missionary. The next day, we flew to Balimo.

No one knew we were coming, and neither of us knew anyone in Balimo. When we arrived at the airport, it was quite a shock to the people that Americans would show up. But someone there remembered seeing him on his first trip, and he was with Roy Biyama's truck. He said hi to Dale and asked what brought him back to Balimo. Dale told him that he had come to bring a missionary, me, so I could learn where I was to start the mission project. Then he introduced me. The guy told Dale and me to get into his truck and he drove us to the village to meet Roy Biyama.

When Roy heard that Dale and I had arrived, he also was in shock; only two weeks earlier he had decided to close his store on the Sabbath, and here was a Seventh-day Adventist missionary showing up in his village.

It took Roy about two seconds to say to me, "You are my missionary." The only houses in Balimo that were not already occupied were his four new government houses and Roy lost no time in saying that my family would be staying in one of them. Had we arrived one month earlier, the houses would not have been ready and he would not have started closing his stores on the Sabbath yet. If we had arrived one month later, they would already have been rented out to government workers. God definitely sent our family at exactly the right time He needed us to arrive in PNG.

The style home Roy Biyama built for us in Balimo

The next day, Dale and I flew back to Port Moresby so I could pick up my family. I asked if we could visit his mission project before heading to Balimo, and he said yes. After beginning the journey toward Dowa, we had to get off the flatbed truck so we could travel by river to his village. More than a hundred people were there, also waiting for people with canoes to transport them somewhere. But no one was there to take anyone. As we waited for someone who could take us, several men started walking around our family dozens of times. I did not know what they were planning to do, but then all of a sudden, they just left.

Not too much longer, one person showed up and said, "I can take you." We were the only people who got a canoe that night. After leaving Dale Goodson's mission project, the police told us we needed to ride with them on their boat in a different direction to get back to the truck because too much crime was taking place in that area where those men had been walking around our family. That is when I learned what those men walking around us was most likely about; God saved us.

Just a few days after my entire family arrived in Balimo at the Gogodala project, Bobbi and I were walking down the main dirt street, and she heard an American accent coming from across the dirt road. I was headed to meet with Roy, Bobbi wife decided to go over to investigate the American accent. What she learned was, they were a missionary couple from another denomination in America, visiting Balimo.

When they saw my wife, they asked her how she had gotten to Balimo. She replied, "By plane." "No," they said, "we mean how did you get permission to come here?" Bobbi then learned that they had been trying for five years to come to Balimo to work as missionaries and were never given permission. They could not find any place to live because no one would rent to them, and actually, there were no houses to rent. They were there trying again, and without success, were leaving that afternoon to fly back to Port Moresby.

Of the 1,000 people who lived in Balimo, not one person wanted a missionary to come to their town, except for Roy Biyama. And it just so happened that it was Roy who owned the first new home to be built in Balimo in 22 years. And Roy would *never* let me pay him rent to live in the new home where we stayed for our first six months of the Gogodala mission project.

CHAPTER 5

TEACHER ALICE

After leaving Grand Rapids, Michigan, where I had been teaching for the previous four years, I missed my students. When we arrived in Balimo, I found that there was a teacher at the government elementary school, Daniel Sewanene, who was an Adventist; he was also the school's principal. He had left the Middle Fly District to become a teacher, and, during that time, he met some Adventists and was baptized. I met one other man, Judah, who was an Adventist. He was not a Gogodala person, but his wife, Grace, was. Judah worked for the government in Balimo.

Because Daniel was a Gogodala person, he was the one to teach me how to speak the Gogodala language. The first thing he taught me was how to say *good morning, how are you doing*.

About a month after we had arrived in Balimo, I decided that I needed to do something for my students back in America. I wanted to see if I could take a video of a class in session in

Balimo and send it to my students in America so they could see what it would be like if they were learning at a school in PNG.

So one morning, I walked over to the elementary school and met with Daniel. I asked whether I could see if any teachers would let me take a video of them and their students. He said yes, I could, if the teachers would let me. Their school was a lot different from our schools in America. They had no more than two classrooms per building. There were classrooms on one side of their property, and classrooms on the other side. As I was leaving his office, walking down between them, I noticed a classroom that had been built only about one year before we arrived. It was built like a bush house. It was one room, and the outside wall was only about four feet tall. I could see the teacher and all the kids in the room.

I immediately decided that that was the first teacher I was going to ask about creating a video. It was the kindergarten class and Alice was the teacher. I stopped and stood at the entrance into the classroom. Alice saw me and invited me in and asked what I needed. I told her about wanting to create a video of her teaching and she said, yes, I could do that, but not that day. She said, "Come back tomorrow and do it then." I learned later that the reason she told me to come back the next day; after I left, she told the kids what I was going to do and that they needed to wear their best clothes the following day.

When I showed up, I took the video and she even had the kids sing some songs. It was amazing what she did for me. After I left, I immediately mailed the video back to my students at Grand Rapids Junior Academy. About two weeks later, I needed to ask Daniel something else, so I headed back to his office. As I was walking past Alice's classroom, I noticed that there was not one student there. But Alice was sitting on one of her desks by the entrance and saw me walking on their property, so I went over to meet her again and thank her for the video.

After I told her I had already mailed it back to America, she asked, "The next time you travel to Port Moresby, would you get me a book?" I replied, "Yes, I could do that." I asked her what the title was. Her response was, "I don't remember the name of the book." I was very confused. How could someone ask me to pick them up a book but not know the title of it? While she was still talking about it, I figured I would just tell her that when she could remember the title then I would get it for her.

But then she told me that a week earlier she was listening to a radio program where some guy recommended the book. Because I assumed it might have been Adventist World Radio (AWR) she was listening to, I asked her the name of the show she'd heard. All she could tell me was that it was a show she'd never heard before and, for some reason, it just showed up. I decided I should start guessing the book she might want, and said, "Was it *The Great Controversy*?" She responded, "Yes, that is the book!"

I was amazed that God had led me to pick the one book in the world that she wanted. I told her I would be glad to get her one, and after our discussion, I did not even go see Daniel. Instead, I went to Judah, to see if the government had a phone that I could use to make a call. When I arrived, he told me that the government did have one phone and it was actually in his office. He told me that it didn't always work, but yes, I could use it.

The person I needed to call was Les Anderson, a missionary in Africa who had become a pilot so he could travel more easily to his mission projects. When we arrived in PNG, he was the person in charge of the Adventist Aviation department in Goroka, which was in the highlands. They are said to have the most favorable climate in all the world. At the 5,000-foot elevation, the weather is mild, and the soil is good for crops. They had what they called the ten-toea market. A toea is like a penny in PNG; one hundred equal one kina. Almost anything you wanted to buy at that food market was only ten toea.

Because he was also an American, I wanted to call him to see where in PNG I could buy a copy of *The Great Controversy*. When I called, he answered immediately. I had expected to talk to one of his employees, but he was not actually flying right then, so I was able to get through to him directly.

He told me that the best place to purchase the book was at the union conference office there in PNG. Because they had books on sale, I could get *The Great Controversy, The Desire of Ages*, and *Steps to Christ,* all for just five kina. He also mentioned that on the following day, Tuesday, he was actually flying down to the union conference office, so if I wanted, he would pick up some books for me. I told him, "Yes, please do that, and pick up three sets of them." Then he told me one more thing. He said that on Thursday or maybe Friday, he was also heading to Daru in Western Province, and flying over our village, so he could drop off the books at the airport in Balimo, which was created during World War II.

On Wednesday, I decided to go see Judah again to call Les Anderson to see if he knew the exact day and time he would arrive in Balimo. It would take close to two hours to walk to the airport, so I needed to know when to leave. Judah said I could use his phone again, but it did not work. I tried a couple more times and it still didn't work. I eventually learned that it almost never worked again the entire five years I worked as a missionary in PNG. But God did make it work, to order Alice's book.

I had no idea when to go to the airport, so I just did not go. Then on Friday, some man met me on our main street in

Balimo; he told me that a plane showed up when he was at the airport, and the pilot asked if he would take some boxes to me. I took them and brought a set to Alice, and immediately she started reading *The Great Controversy*.

A few months later, after we had moved to another village, Alice was in the Balimo hospital. It was not a hospital like the ones we are used to in more developed countries. They had no running water or electricity. The did not even have any doctors. But they did have a roof over their heads and windows, and they had nurses. Alice was suffering from asthma and was having a hard time breathing. The nurses were trying to insert an IV, but just couldn't find a vein. As Alice lay there thinking she was going to die from lack of oxygen, she felt that she was being led to accept the Sabbath. Eventually she said, "Okay, God! I accept, I accept the Sabbath, and I will keep it."

Immediately the nurse found a vein and inserted the needle so they could administer the medication she needed, and she started breathing again. Because God had her listen to AWR, and led me to meet with her and even know what book she wanted, and because Les Anderson agreed to deliver the book, she was able to save her life by accepting the Sabbath. I learned that all of this had just happened one day as I happened to travel to Balimo. Alice then asked me how she could attend our church.

Because Daniel's family would meet with Judah and his family at Judah's house on the Sabbath and on Wednesday night for prayer meeting, I told him that Alice wanted to join them. Alice began attending their church meetings every Sabbath, along with her two sons and daughter. But on the Sabbath, her husband, Joseph, who worked for the government, would put on his rough clothes and meet up with friends early in the morning to go drink alcohol.

Then, one Sabbath, as Alice's children got up and began to get ready for church, they were shocked to see their father wearing his good clothes. They could not understand why he would wear his good clothes to go out drinking with his friends. One of the kids asked why he had his good clothes on, and his response was, "Because I am going to church with you today." They were so excited to hear that.

If you worked for the government, once every three years they would send you back to your home village to meet with your family members. Because Joseph worked for the government, it got to be time for him to travel back to his home village. He told me what he was going to do when he arrived there. He said, "I am going to be a fisher of men." He was going to share with his home village members what he had learned—what his wife had read in Ellen G. White's book *The Great Controversy*.

CHAPTER 6

NO RAIN

When we arrived in Balimo, we learned that for almost six months, it had not rained even one day. This, of course, was causing problems. There was only one well, and everyone had to go there to get their water. One morning, right after we started living in one of Roy Biyama's new houses, some of his employees showed up with his tractor, pulling a trailer with a water tank on it. They had gone to the well and filled a thousand-gallon tank to bring our family some water.

Because next to his house he had a 3,000-gallon tank that was used to collect rain from the roof, they started giving me water in a five-gallon bucket. I would take the bucket to the tank, climb a tall ladder, and fill it up with their water. I was so thankful that we then had water right at our house.

The other problem for the Gogodala people was that they were not getting enough to eat. None of the twenty-five villages could get their gardens to produce much. But the worst thing was that their sago trees were no longer growing, either. After cutting down a sago tree, the men would strip off the outer bark and then the women would pound the sago palm. Then they would place the pounded sago into bags made of woven grass. By pouring water through the bags and then stepping on them, the women washed the starch out of the bags on top of some plastic tarps. The modern plastic tarps worked well to hold the water and starch. After a few minutes, the starch would settle out of the water and collect on the bottom on the tarp. They were always doing this because sago was their main food. But they were even losing sago, too.

Roy Biyama could not even order any more food for his grocery store; because the Aramia River had dropped almost twenty-five feet, the cargo ships could no longer deliver his products from Port Moresby. One day he told me something interesting. One thing did arrive on an airplane—sugar. The people of Gogodola loved hot chocolate, but their cocoa powder mix was unsweetened, contain, so sugar was very important to them.

Our family would travel to Port Moresby to buy food, so we did not have much of an issue. But as it got close to ten months with no rain, we were almost out of food, too. One day, I walked to Roy Biyama's store to buy some rice. When I arrived, they told me that they no longer had any. Because Roy was my best friend in Balimo, I walked to the back of his store to ask how we could get some rice. Roy was not there, but as I was asking one of his employees about getting rice, someone else heard my request and told me that they did have one bag; it had broken open and they could not sell it, but I was free to take it.

I asked how much it would cost, and he told me nothing, just take it. It was a twenty-pound bag, and I started carrying it down the dirt road back to our house. As I was walking, a man met me and said, "Where did you find that rice, can I have some of it?" I told him what had happened and gave him some for his family. As I started walking again, someone else showed up and asked the same thing. So I gave him some, too. Before I got home, four men asked if I could give them some of the rice, and I did. When I got home, only half of the bag was left.

A couple of weeks later, the elementary school was having their graduation day. Because Australia and PNG are in the southern hemisphere, their summer months are December, January, and February, so the school graduation party fell in November. That was just five months after we had arrived in PNG. For some reason, I was asked if I would say the prayer for the graduation party. When it was time for me to pray, I walked up to the platform and started praying for the students, the teachers, and the parents.

Then for some reason, I started wondering whether I should also include in my prayer the Gogodala people's need for rain. That had nothing to do with the school, but I decided I needed to add that to my prayer. So I asked God if He would send us back His rain. The very next day, we had the first rain in Gogodala in eleven months. Then the rain started coming back as it had always been. God provided for their needs!

CHAPTER 7

WHERE WERE WE SUPPOSED TO LIVE?

When we arrived in Balimo in July of 1997, I had been told by AFM that the first thing I needed to do was learn the Gogodala language. Because Daniel was teaching me, I began to wonder where I was supposed to live to actually start showing people how to follow Jesus. I wondered whether I was supposed to stay in Balimo, the government center, or to travel to one of the other twenty-four villages up and down the Aramia River where all thirty-five thousand Gogodala people lived. Every morning when I woke up, the first thought I had was how am I ever going to know where God wants me to live, to start the Gogodala mission project.

A few months after we arrived, someone from a village called Kotale showed up in Balimo with the message that some people from his village wanted to come and meet with me.

I said yes, so they scheduled a trip from Kotale to Balimo. It would take an hour and a half to travel down the Aramia River in a dugout canoe with an outboard motor. But it was going to take them closer to several hours to paddle from Kotale to Balimo. When they arrived, it was Tomas, Wolfy, and Wolfy's wife who arrived. They brought some food and cooked it for our family and them. When we were finished eating, one of them asked if I would move to their village. I did not know why they wanted me to move there, but I assumed there had to be some reason, so I said yes, we could move to Kotale Village.

After agreeing to move to Kotale Village, I learned several interesting things. Back when a young boy named Jack Mulaki was in the seventh grade, his cousin Bob Daniya was in the eighth grade. Both of their families were members of the Evangelical Church of PNG, and both boys wanted to become pastors for their church. When they asked the church if they could become pastors when they grew up, Bob was told that he could become a pastor, and Jack was told that he could not. Jack was very upset that they would not let him become a pastor. Because his father worked for the government, he was able to leave the Gogodala people and move to the highlands to attend high school in a village near Adventist Aviation.

Eventually he decided that if his church would not let him become a pastor, then it could not be God's true church. He began studying the other denominations that had churches in PNG, and he became a Seventh-day Adventist. Eventually, he decided that he needed to travel back to his village and share the Sabbath with them. When he arrived, he asked the chief to hold a meeting with the entire village, and the chief agreed. After Jack shared the Sabbath with them, he asked if anyone would be willing to keep the Sabbath. Two men raised their hands, Tomas and Wolfy.

Jack then donated some property to the Seventh-day Adventist Church, and he had a young boy named Kadu plant two bushes to show the size of the property. Next, Jack convinced someone from the Highlands to move to his village and start a church. The individual did build a church, but for some reason had to leave and could not start the church. Then one Sabbath, Tomas walked to the church and was reading his Bible there. He decided to pray that God would send his village a Seventh-day Adventist missionary. When I learned that he did that, I asked him when he said that prayer. It turned out that it was very close to the time when our family decided to become missionaries and AFM asked us to start the Gogodala mission project in PNG.

Of all twenty-five Gogodala villages, not one village had anyone who wanted SDA missionaries, or had any property for our church, except for Kotale Village.

Of all twenty-five Gogodala villages, not one village had anyone who wanted SDA missionaries, or had any property for our church, except for Kotale Village. After we moved there, I was told that the ECP church had a camp meeting one weekend, from Friday to Sunday, and the seven villages that were the closest to Kotale attended. I was also told that they did not say one word about God the entire meeting, but talked only about what they needed to do to force our family to leave the Gogodala project. That also showed me that God definitely wanted our family to move to Kotale Village.

The man whose father met with the angel about the seven days

One other thing that had happened in Kotale was that an old man told me that when he was a young boy, his father had met with an angel The angel told his father to find a tree branch with multiple leaves on it. The angel then told the man to break the branch so that there were only seven leaves on it. He then told him to take one leaf off on the first day. Then in the morning on the second day, to take a second one off. He was to do that every day, and when he took off the sixth leaf, he was to tell the people to collect their coconuts, their fish, and any food they needed. Then the angel told him that when the seventh day arrived, and he removed the seventh leaf, he needed to tell the people to rest at home. Then in the 1930s, some European missionaries arrived and were very impressed that the Kotale Village people were honoring one day a week. But they told them it needed to be the following day, Sunday, and the people made the change. Then in 1966, Some missionaries from Australia founded the Evangelical Church of Papua New Guinea (ECP) among the Gogodala people.

All of these stories that I eventually heard proved to me that God did indeed send us to Kotale Village to start the Gogodala mission project.

The bush house Tomas was building for us in Kotale Village

CHAPTER 8

NO FOOD

Because we agreed to move to Kotale Village, Tomas began building us a bush house. One day, he was planning to travel by canoe out in the creeks to pick up some wood to work on it. He had informed three men, Raymond, Nasa, and Wolfy, that he needed them to come with him, and they agreed. That same day, I had made a trip from Balimo to meet with Raymond in Kotale. Raymond and his wife, Aina, were the first people our family had met with in Kotale Village on our first trip there. We had stayed in their house for two days on our first visit a few weeks earlier.

Out outdoor house (bathroom) at our bush house

When I arrived, I learned that Tomas and those three men were planning to travel to get some wood for our house. I told Raymond that I would like to travel with them, too. Raymond agreed, but then a couple of hours later, I was informed that they had canceled the trip, and I could return to Balimo.

A few hours after deciding to return to Balimo, I heard that Tomas had changed his mind and was again planning to travel for the wood., I notified Tomas that I would stay and would still like to go with them. Eventually I learned that Tomas was afraid that if I went with them, I might get hurt some-how; that was why he had canceled the trip and expected me to return to Balimo. After he had twice changed his plan, I was finally able

> *Eventually I learned that Tomas was afraid that if I went with them, I might get hurt somehow; that was why he had canceled the trip and expected me to return to Balimo.*

to convince Tomas that there was no problem with my traveling with them, and that I really wanted to go.

In the end, Raymond persuaded Tomas to let me go with them. So the next morning, we headed for the woods down the creek—almost a two-hour trip—and it was the first time ever that I drank the same water the Gogodala people drank. Until then, I had always been given water from the tank; Bobbi had it filtered before any of us would drink it. But I was not affected, and that surprised me.

The day before I had left Balimo to visit Raymond, I had told my family that I would be gone for only two days. I had left them enough money to buy food from Roy's store. But because Tomas and his friends had decided to make the trip to get the wood, I was gone from Balimo longer than expected. Because of the extra two days, my family had spent all of their money on Tuesday, and on Wednesday they had no food or money.

That morning, my wife and our daughters knelt down on the floor and prayed that God would help them solve their problem of having no food. A few hours later, a woman my family did not know showed up at the house with a bag of food to give them. It was Alice, the teacher who I had taken the video of with her students, who had asked me for a copy of *The Great Controversy*.

As Alice said hi to Bobbi, she asked if she liked "proons." Bobbi said yes and thanked Alice for bringing them the food. She then set the bag down in the kitchen and then she and our daughters headed down the dirt road to Grace and Judah's home where the four Seventh-day Adventists who lived in Balimo would meet for church and Wednesday evening prayer meeting.

After they finished the prayer meeting, Grace and her husband, Judah, told my family that they would walk with them back to our house since it was after dark and they wanted to make sure they would be safe. When they arrived at our house, they all went inside, and Stacy and Rachel headed to the kitchen to see what Alice had given them for supper. As they entered the kitchen, they were shocked. The bag was moving. They ran out into the living room and told Bobbi what they had just seen.

Bobbi was surprised at seeing a bag of food moving, so Grace joined her and picked up the bag. To her surprise, she found some prawns in it. A prawn is a marine crustacean that resembles a large shrimp, many varieties of which are edible. Bobbi then realized that she had misunderstood Alice's question; she thought Alice had said *prune*, but she actually had said *prawn*. It was laughable, the way she misunderstood Alice's language.

Grace told Bobbi that she probably should return the prawns to Alice and let her know that they could not eat that meat because of the Bible's description of clean and unclean animals. The last thing that she found in the bag was twenty kina. Alice, apparently, was God's means of answering my family's prayer for food that day. Two days later, I arrived back home in Balimo and learned how God had taken care of my family.

CHAPTER 9

CRATE

Because it was now close to the end of December of 1997, we were ready to move to Kotale Village. But I had a question. Should I move there before I found the crate that I had created back in America to ship our house supplies to PNG? I created a wood crate on a pallet that was four feet wide, eight feet long, and six feet tall, covered with plywood. Into the crate we had put our clothes, our appliances, my tools, and a non-electric hand-crank laundry-washing device. I did not know why it had not shown up yet, in almost six months, so I decided to travel back to Port Moresby to find it before we would move to Kotale Village.

When we arrived in Port Moresby, the government told me that it had not shown up yet. But then someone at Pacific Adventist University told me that there were a couple of ware-houses there that I should check out. The first one said that they did not have the crate. But at the second, a man checked out the back of the warehouse and returned saying, "Yes, we have it in the back."

For some reason, it had been put in the back of their warehouse and they did not forward it. But then he told me they could not give it to me because they had to send it to the import department, which would have to examine everything in the crate and calculate the cost, to charge me taxes for it. He informed me that it would be done in a month or two.

That Sabbath I attended the University's church, and right before the sermon was preached, someone stood up and told the congregation that they had a guest speaker named John Pundari. He said that everyone needed to know that John had just a few months earlier been elected as the speaker of parliament. The position is similar to the speaker of the house in America. After John Pundari finished his sermon, he walked out of the church and stood by the door to shake people's hands.

Me and John Pundari in 2011 on a later visit to PNG

When I got there, he shook my hand but then turned his head to the left and was no longer looking at me, but was still holding my hand. Then in a few seconds he looked back at me and said, "Thank you so much for starting the Gogodala mission project out in Western Province!"

What I learned was that he had an uncle standing behind him, telling him what I was doing there in PNG. His uncle was actually attending the university so he could go to the seminary to become an ordained pastor. John asked his uncle if he would bring me to the capital to meet with him. He said he could, and asked if I would be willing to come. I was very excited to meet someone that high in the government so I said, "Yes, I will." He told his uncle to pick me up at 10:00 a.m. on Monday and bring me to his office.

Me and John Pundari's entire family in Port Moresby

On Monday morning I was ready by 9:00 a.m., but the uncle never showed up. I thought, oh well, no problem. Then on

Wednesday morning, because our family needed more food, I walked to the back of the university to the farm where they grew fruits and vegetables to sell to grocery stores in the city. It was only on Wednesdays and Fridays that people at the university could buy food there. After I picked up what we needed, I was walking to the checkout area when I saw a guy who had been working on the farm enter the building.

He saw me and said, "Oh, Jeff, I am so sorry. I forgot I was supposed to take you to the capital to meet with my nephew John. Do you want me to call him back and see if he still wants me to bring you to see him?" I said, "Yes, if you want to give him a call." John told his uncle to bring me there on Thursday, so we arrived the next day. John showed me his offices and we talked. The most interesting comment he made was that when the people voted for a law, he was the one who signed it to make it legal, something our president does here in America. Then he told his uncle that he wanted to show me around the city.

We climbed into John's personal car, and just about two minutes after we started driving, his uncle said, "John, this guy needs the crate he sent from America here approved. Can you help him?" Because John had a car phone in his car, he told his uncle to look up the number in his phone book and dial the import department.

Someone answered and John said, "Hello, my name is John Pundari, I am your newly elected speaker of parliament. Do you have Jeff Bishop's name on your list for items shipped here from foreign countries?" The person said, "Yes, we do have him on our list." Then John asked if he could take care of it for me, a missionary. The guy asked John what was in the crate. I told John, and he relayed the information. Then John said, "Thank you for working on this matter, and have a good day."

About an hour later we arrived back at the capital, and John told his uncle that because he had to go back to work, he should just take me back to the university, which was about fourteen miles away. When we arrived, he parked his car next to the main office building. Instantly someone showed up and said, "About half an hour to forty-five minutes ago, the government delivered this *huge* crate we have no way to keep here. What can I do with it?" We both were so excited that it was already there, and I was charged no taxes. I told them they could deliver it right away to the coastal shipping department at Fairfax Harbor, from where my friend Roy Biyama would bring it to Balimo for me.

The next time we traveled to Port Moresby, I again needed to buy food. But it was not Wednesday, so I went to a small-format grocery store beside the university library. When I left the store and was walking out to the street to head back to our apartment, John Pundari appeared and said to me, "Why didn't you tell me you were back in Port Moresby?" (I didn't know I was supposed to do that.) He continued, "Whenever you come to Port Moresby, let me know you are here so we can get together." He actually wanted to be my friend. Over the five years that followed, each time I went to Port Moresby, we would meet and do a lot of things together, including playing basketball at his friend's home. And every time, he would give a donation to our mission project. Then two years later, when he became the deputy prime minister (similar to the position of vice president in America), he told me he would be able to donate even more, and promised to give me twenty thousand kina.

A while later, my aunt Judy and our daughter Stacy, who had returned to America to attend college, spent a week visiting us in PNG. After aunt Judy headed home, our family traveled for a visit to another part of PNG. While we were there, we went to a restaurant for lunch. A newspaper was there, so I began reading it. I was shocked. It gave the news that John Pundari had been fired from his position as deputy prime minister. The following day we traveled back to Port Moresby and, because I was upset that my friend had been fired, I drove to his best friend's house to find him. When I arrived, I knocked on the door of John's best friend's house and asked his wife if John was there and she said, "Yes, he is, he is at the kitchen table." I then entered the house and as I met with John, his first words were, "Sorry, Jeff, I can no longer donate the twenty thousand kina to your mission project."

I was surprised he was more sorry about being unable to donate to the Gogodala mission project than about being fired as deputy prime minister. I learned that someone had lied to the prime minister about him, and that was why he was fired. But for the rest of the time we lived in PNG, John and I always got together when I traveled to Port Moresby.

CHAPTER 10

HENRY AND MALAWATO

On a Thursday afternoon, after God had solved our crate issue, we flew back to Balimo. We were ready to move to Kotale Village on Friday, but that did not work out. The weather had been very bad for almost a whole year. It was raining again, but because there had not been any rain for the ten previous months, the river had dropped over twenty feet. Our normal route to Kotale Village was to turn north off of the Aramia River and onto a creek just past Kewa Village. But that creek had dried a long way from the village, so we had to use a different creek farther up the Aramia. I was not familiar with that route, so a friend told me he would take us there in our boat, but he could not do it on Friday.

So on Sabbath morning, we headed to Kotale Village in the new direction. When we arrived, something very interesting was going on; some people in the church were celebrating the Sabbath. I had no idea that the church was already started. But then I learned something else.

There was a lady named Malawato who grew up in Kotale Village. She had become a nurse, and was working at a hospital somewhere in the North Fly district. She had married a man named Henry who had grown up in the North Fly District. Because Henry was a Seventh-day Adventist, Malawato became one, too.

After we arrived in Balimo, they showed up there, too, and met with us. Malawato was then a nurse in Balimo. Malawato would often arrive at our house and play games with my wife and daughters out on our deck. The reason they traveled back to Balimo was that when they were living in the North Fly District, some people from another village were looking to kill Henry. You see, in PNG, if someone kills a person from another village, the victim's village will retaliate by killing someone from the killer's village. What happened was, someone from Henry's village had just killed someone in the village where he and Malawato were living, and the victim's village decided to make Henry the object of their vengeance killing.

> *What happened was, someone from Henry's village had just killed someone in the village where he and Malawato were living, and the victim's village decided to make Henry the object of their vengeance killing.*

The moment he found out, Henry ran down to a creek and put something on his head so no one could see him. He immersed himself in the water except for his mouth, so that he could breathe. He actually stayed in that creek for two days while Malawato scheduled a flight back to Balimo. That is what brought them back to the Gogodala villages.

> *God apparently sent Henry and Malawato back to the Gogodala villages so His Church would be started in Kotale Village as soon as our family arrived there.*

Because Henry knew we were moving to Kotale Village after traveling back to Port Moresby for our crate, he felt that he had to start our church before we arrived in Kotale Village. So they traveled back to Malawato's village two weeks before we arrived there and started the church. That is why it was already established that first day we arrived in Kotale. God apparently sent Henry and Malawato back to the Gogodala villages so His Church would be started in Kotale Village as soon as our family arrived there. I began preaching there the very next Sabbath.

Because I was supposed to be preaching sermons in the Gogodala language, one Sabbath I asked whether they needed me to start preaching in their language. But they all responded, "No, we want to learn more English!" So every Sabbath I would preach, and Raymond would interpret in Gogodala for those who did not know English well enough, so they could learn more English. Most people in Kotale Village did know English. In fact, English is used in the schools in PNG.

Our dog who we named Gordy

CHAPTER 11

OUR FIRST TIME
IN KOTALE VILLAGE

When we did arrive back in Balimo after getting my crate approved, Roy Biyama notified me when his cargo ship was planning to arrive with the crate so that I could bring some dugout canoes to take the supplies to Kotale Village where we were finally living. Because of the lack of rain of the previous year, the lake near our bush house was much lower, causing the distance to be much farther than it usually was. Fortunately, dozens of kids wanted to help, so we had enough assistance carrying all of the supplies to our house.

That is how the people noticed the aspirin, the antiacids, the quinine, and the medicine that would work for their health issues. They also saw bandages and charcoal, and a few other items we had loaded in our pallet. Then someone asked me if the aspirin were just for Seventh-day Adventists. My response was, "No, they are for anyone with medical issues." The following day, people began showing up to be treated for all kinds of medical issues including kids who had cut their skin and wanted treatment.

The children loved to come and visit Stacy and Rachel. They would show our girls all of the sores on their bodies, even teeny tiny ones. Our daughters would give them a bandage or small amounts of triple antibiotic cream. Then sometimes the kids would walk a short distance away, pull off their scabs, and then return to have them fixed again. They loved to touch Stacy and Rachel's skin and rub their hair. They could not understand why our daughters did not have any bugs in their hair. Those children loved our daughters.

One other thing we treated people for was malaria. I had been informed that if someone had a fever, we needed to give them hydroxychloroquine. I was told that I did not need to confirm that they had malaria to give them the medicine because it didn't matter. Eventually, someone in the village commented that people from every other village were traveling to the hospital in Balimo and dying, but no one from Kotale Village was dying. People weren't even dying from snake bites because of the supplies we had been able to bring with us.

When we were preparing to head to PNG, we learned about a device similar to a taser that can change the shape of the snake venom enzymes and proteins so that the venom would no longer harm the person. We would touch the spot where the snake had bitten, and turn the taser on for two seconds. Then we would move it around the bite and turn it back on twice more. It took three times to completely destroy the venom.

On one trip from Balimo back to Kotale Village, Bobbi, Rachel, and I were bringing a young girl with us. When we had arrived in Kotale Village after dark, we began walking to our house. The young girl was leading us, Rachel was following her, I was behind Rachel, and Bobbi was behind me.

All of a sudden, the young girl fell to the ground; she had been bitten on her leg by a snake. We helped the girl get to our house and I treated her with that taser. I wrapped her leg and took her home. The next morning, as I was walking down the trail in Kotale Village, I passed her house. As soon as she saw me, she jumped down the stairs and, smiling, gave me back the wraps that I had put on her leg. She was so happy and thankful for what we had done to prevent her from dying from that snake bite. In less than a day, she was completely healthy.

My wife began praying that God would not allow this man to be able to do anything if he were a witch doctor.

One time when I was traveling in PNG, one of Wolfy's sons, Ganooba, had been bitten by a snake, and it took his friends several hours to get him back to the village to see us. Bobbi got out the taser and started treating Ganooba. All of a sudden, a man showed up and entered our house and knelt down by Ganooba. He appeared to be praying or communicating with some spirits.

Bobbi was concerned that he might be a witch doctor. The Gogodala people had a lot of witch doctors. They believed that a person could decide whether to be the type that sent snakes to kill people or the type who went to save people from being bitten by a snake. My wife began praying that God would not allow this man to be able to do anything if he were a witch doctor.

The man said that he could not do anything, so he left our house. After treating Ganooba with the taser, Bobbi wrapped his leg and then asked the men if they would like something to eat. They agreed, so she made some rice and decided to feed them the fish that she was cooking. People would often drop off fish for us, to say thank you for what we were doing for them. But most of the time we would just cook the fish and feed them to our dog, Gordy. When these men arrived, the fish in the oven were being cooked for Gordy, but now it was a good idea to use the fish to feed these men.

Bobbi put the fish on a plate with the rice and served the men. As they finished eating, she noticed that they all had put the fish's scales on the plates. Because everyone knows everything about everyone in Kotale Village, the next morning someone brought Bobbi some more fish and told her, "You need to remove the scales on these fish before you eat them."

During our five years serving as missionaries with the Gogodala people, we saved nine people who had been bitten by snakes; no one in our village died from a snake bite the entire time.

What did happen, however, about a month after we arrived in Kotale Village, was that someone told me I *had* to leave. They did not want a missionary in their village. I went to our village chief and told him what was going on and asked him what I needed to do. He said he would have a village meeting for us.

When the meeting started, everyone was standing out in front of our bush house. During the meeting, someone said, "We can't prove this property belonged to Jack Mulaki, so they can't live here!" Another man responded, "If we are still trying to prove who owns what property, then you women have to stop making sago for your families because we can't prove those trees are on your property, either." Immediately the women got upset and frustrated.

Only women could make sago. The village chief was then able to calm them down and he asked a question. "Do we need to tell these people they need to leave Kotale Village?" Immediately, every person responded, "Owa." That is the Gogodala word for *no*. They all decided that we did not have to leave. I wondered then if it was because of that person who had asked me if our medicine was just for Adventists and I responded by saying it was for anyone who needed it; maybe that led to people coming every day for help. Maybe the way we helped improve their lives was what convinced them that they wanted us to remain in Kotale Village.

Doing health checks to anyone who needed it in Kotale village; because of this the people said "Awa" NO—we do not want them to have to leave Kotale village

CHAPTER 12

DREAM

When we arrived in Balimo, a woman whose son who had passed away told people I was her son come back to life. She told everyone that she was giving me her son's Gogodala name, Ba:kele (beh-kay-lay). That wasn't true because when we die, we are asleep until Jesus returns, but that is how I got my Gogodala name, Ba:kele.

What is interesting is that when a Gogodala person has a Gogodala name but someone wants to give them a nickname, they use English. There was a nineteen-year-old boy named Nasa, but the Kotale Village actually called him Nasty. They called him Nasty because they thought he was a nasty young man. He was a drug dealer and a thief, and not always nice. His dad had a nickname, too, Taxi. They called him Taxi because he was a player in the rugby league. In America, we would call him a football player. Whenever he was running for a touchdown and someone tried to tackle him, he would just carry them. I was told that he would even carry two people at a time, trying to tackle him.

After Henry and Malawato had moved to Balimo, Malawato told Henry that Taxi was in the hospital with his daughter, who was very ill. I had not yet met Taxi, but Henry told me one time when I was traveling to Balimo on my plastic dinghy with an outboard motor that we needed to go to the hospital to meet with Taxi. It was Roy Biyama who had taught me how to work that dinghy so I could travel up and down the Aramia River. So Henry and I went to see Taxi and his daughter. Taxi shared a lot of information with me, and I prayed for him and his daughter. Then Henry prayed, too, and also gave Taxi a Bible.

The following morning, when Taxi's daughter woke up, she told her dad she'd had a very interesting dream. He told her to tell him about it. She said that in her dream she was walking down the dirt road in Balimo and when she arrived at the end of the road, she saw her older brother headed in some direction carrying a five-gallon bucket of water. Then she told him that she also saw that American guy they had met the day before (me) walking in the opposite direction. He, too, was carrying a five-gallon bucket of water.

In her dream, she went to see her brother, and when she got to him, she noticed that his water was filthy. She said that she would not ever drink that water. Then she decided to walk in the opposite direction and meet with me. When she arrived, she noticed the water in my bucket and told her dad that it was 100 percent pure, clean water. That made Taxi very interested to learn why his daughter had that dream, so he told his two younger sons, Nasa and Gamani, to go see that American, and find out what he was doing.

Because I was the pastor at our Kotale Village church, they decided to come listen to my sermon. I was surprised that the two young men had come to our church. The following week, they came back again, and then kept coming every Sabbath. Then one afternoon, about three months later, I took a walk down through our village. When I was about a half mile from our house, I decided to continue down the hill to see a house that was near the lake.

Then I headed back up the hill and all of a sudden someone was walking from the other side of the hill towards me. I realized it was Nasa. We kept walking toward each other and when we arrived at the same spot, he raised his right hand for a high-five. I raised my left hand and we had a high-five. He said, "I do believe in God! I want to follow Jesus."

We pulled our arms down, but he kept hold of my hand. I told him we should walk back to my house and I would share with him what he needed to know. For the entire walk, he held my hand. A few weeks later, Gamani told me that he, too, wanted to join our church. He said that he'd had a dream, too: He and I were walking on a beach near a lake, when he saw my footprints in the sand and decided to walk behind me, in my footprints behind me. That convinced him he wanted to walk in the same direction as I, was, toward Jesus. Nasa and Gamani were the first two people in Kotale Village to tell me that they wanted to become members of our church.

Ray Hobson, professor at University

CHAPTER 13

TAKE A BREAK

One of the first things AFM told me upon our arrival at PNG was that we would need to take a break every three months. They actually said we had to travel to somewhere else in PNG every three months, and just relax and have some fun. Several times we went to Port Moresby to buy some things. There was a very nice professor at Pacific Adventist University in Port Moresby, Ray Hobson, who was from Australia, and he would let us stay with him and his wife while we were in Port Moresby. He even told me that for the entire week we were there, I could use his little diesel truck to drive into the city.

During one of our visits, Bobbi and I drove to a strip mall to buy several items. The national post office was there, along with our bank and several stores, all on the same property. There was a large parking lot between the post office and the stores. The bank was in the middle.

Because we needed several items and food, we walked to the large building that had about six stores connected to it, and started our shopping. Because I did not want anyone to see how much cash I had in my pockets, I would always put just the amount I expected to need in one pocket and give that to the cashier as we were checking out. We left the first store with about four bags and then entered the second store. Then after leaving that one, we had a couple more bags and went to the next store.

By the time we left the third store, we were carrying a lot of bags, but we needed only one more item, so we kept heading down the mall. All of a sudden, some man who had been standing at the entrance of a store we were passing, stepped out and raised his hand to shake mine. He said, "Hi Jeff, good to see you! I will help you take your stuff to your car."

I did not need his help, and I did not even know who he was, even though he claimed to know me. He said he knew me through his job at the hospital, where I would go for the medicine we used in caring for our Kotale Village members. After I told him he didn't have to help me, he again said I needed to take the bags to the truck. Again I told him we needed only one more item, so we didn't need his help just yet.

He again said, "Yes, you need to take this to your truck," So I finally decided to just let him do as he wished. Once we got to the truck which was quite a distance from the mall, he explained why he was so intent on getting us back to the truck:

He been listening to five men who were walking behind me, discussing in some PNG language about how they were going to attack me and steal our purchases. He needed to prevent me from being harmed by those men.

Somehow, God actually sent a man from Balimo at exactly the right time to the exact place where those men were planning to attack me. Whether he was really a man who knew me, or an angel who just told me he knew me, I may never know. Either way, God saved us!

> *He been listening to five men who were walking behind me, discussing in some PNG language about how they were going to attack me and steal our purchase.*

CHAPTER 14

SNAKE

When our family first arrived in Kotale Village, the women were very taken with Stacy and Rachel. Even the girls enjoyed being with them at our bush house. Every day the kids would come to see Stacy and Rachel and run their fingers through their hair and rub their arms and legs out of curiosity, as most had never seen white skin before.

The kids also tried to pick lice out of Stacy and Rachel's hair, but I finally told them *muskie*, which is Gogodala for *leave it alone*. It was hard for the kids to find lice in Stacy and Rachel's hair because they did not have any.

Rachel learned how to make sago with the women. Making sago was why the women in Kotale were very strong. A lady once told me that she was worn out from making sago with Rachel because she needed to keep up with Rachel as they were pounding out the sago palm. The women would actually rub Rachel's legs to see how strong she was and then say, "She is truly a Gogodala girl."

Rachel creating sago

Sago was not one of my favorite foods. We did eat a lot of rice, though, since we could buy it in Balimo at Roy's stores. Bobbi also baked homemade bread every day. But one day, we received a care package that contained spaghetti. We were excited to have such a special supper. It arrived just before September 16th, when our family had planned to travel to Balimo in Daniel's large dugout canoe to meet up with some people for the Independence Day celebration.

After the celebration, I brought Bobbi and Rachel and some others back to Kotale Village. Then I had to leave again to pick up a second group of people and bring them back, too. Because of that care package someone had sent us, Bobbi had planned to make the spaghetti as a special treat. But somehow, after it was cooked, it got spilled onto the floor; Bobbi and Rachel were very upset because we had really been looking forward to that special supper.

Me eating sago

As they were cleaning it up, Rachel went to shake her rag outside when suddenly, Bobbi heard her scream and saw her throw the rag and flashlight into the air. Bobbi then ran over with a second light to see what had scared Rachel, and realized that she had just seen a snake coiled up inside our house by the door, right in front of her face.

Bobbi and Rachel debated over which of them should go past the snake to get someone to kill it, and which one should stay and keep track of the snake. Rachel decided she would rather go past the snake than stay there watching it, so she ran out to find someone to come and take care of it.

After the person arrived and got rid of the snake, we learned that snakes that can climb into an elevated house are never poisonous.

CHAPTER 15

LADIES' CONFERENCE

In 1999, the Adventist Union planned a ladies' conference for Western Province, so we informed our church and asked whether any of the women would like to attend. Several were very excited, so we agreed to take them, to it even though most of them had never traveled anywhere outside of their Gogodala villages.

Then one day, I came across a man who had told me that he was one of the local villagers who had eaten the missionary who had been killed at the Fly River dozens of years earlier. He told me that his village had an ocean canoe that we could use to travel from the Fly River down to Daru if we wanted to. Because that would solve our problem of how to get to the conference, I and two other men then planned to travel by river to Daru, with thirty women and their children.

In order to register for the conference, each church member had to fill out a form so the union would know how many people to expect. One of the entries on the form asked the individual's age. Some women who were over fifty years old wrote down that they were thirteen, and some who were twenty years old wrote that they were sixty. They had no idea how old they were.

In order to travel down to Daru Island, we were going to have to raise money for gas for our outboard motor and for food for our time at the conference. I decided to ask Roy Biyama if he would be willing to hire our church members to unload one of his cargo ships and he said yes, he would. Our members unloaded Roy's ship and then prepared for our trip. Roy also said that he would be willing to use his tractor and trailer to haul the ladies and us three men down through the woods—about twenty miles—to the small creek that led to the Fly River. After we reached the creek, we used some local dugout canoes to make it to the village just before the river.

When we arrived, I was concerned because the man who had said he would take us 'to Daru was not in the village, and the boat he had told me about was on the land, not in the water. But as we talked to some of the village members, we learned that there was another man who could also drive the ocean boat down to Daru if we wanted.

When we found that man, he was very interested in taking us because he wanted to go to Daru, too, to buy some things. We agreed to leave the following morning. When I got up, I noticed that the boat was already in the creek. I learned that it was in the water at that time because the sea level was rising. That also explained why it was not in the water when we had arrived; at that part of the day, the sea level had fallen.

That morning, we entered the boat and when we arrived at the Fly River, the wind was creating huge waves, somewhere between seven and ten feet high. The boat would rise and fall. It was a difficult trip, crossing the five-mile-wide river to the other side, where we would head south to the Gulf of Papua.

As we arrived at the gulf, we were a mile from land when we hit the ocean floor and were stuck. But eventually we made it around the southern part of Western Province and down to the island of Daru. It took us seventy-two hours to travel from Balimo to Daru; it took Bobbi and Rachel only twenty minutes by plane.

When we arrived, we set up tents to sleep in. The meetings took place outside on a large grass field, close to where we were staying. Several ladies had small children who were still breastfeeding, so those children also traveled with us to the conference. When the meetings took place, Rachel would stay at the tent to take care of the six little kids who had traveled with their mothers. She made sure they had food and water, and they would sit around the tent and play games. Their favorite was a tag game, where they would run around tagging each other out in the field.

Rachel would convince the kids to follow her and eventually return to the tent. The interesting thing was that when Rachel was out in the field running around with the kids playing, the women sitting in front of the speaker would watch Rachel play with the kids and not pay attention to the speaker. I was actually told by one woman how amazing Rachel was in taking care of the ladies' kids.

When Rachel was at our home church in Kotale Village, she would also play with the kids. During services, some of the little ones would be noisy. Regardless of whether she was in Daru at the women's conference or at our church in Kotale Village, Rachel would not hit or spank any child. Instead, she would just convince them to follow her and do what she asked them to do. During our church service, when some kids would become noisy, she would take them out into the yard and play games with them so that their parents could listen to my sermon. Their favorite game was jacks, which they played with seeds. They loved to play with Rachel and they would often play for hours.

My friend Raymond and his wife, Aina, had a five-year-old son who Rachel played with a lot. One day Aina actually told Rachel that Rachel had taught her how to love her children because of the way she had treated their son.

People traveling in a dugout canoe

CHAPTER 16

RAYMOND

Raymond was born in Kotale Village but later moved with his parents to Daru, the capital city of the Western Province. Raymond committed his first crime in eighth grade when he stole a person's car. Because of his crime, he was not allowed to move forward into high school even though he had gotten the highest score on his final exam in the entire Western Province school district.

One day he met his teacher, who then learned why Raymond could not continue attending school. He told Raymond that he would solve the problem, and he did get Raymond back into school. In order to do that, they had to send Raymond back to the Gogodala Awaba Secondary school on the Aramia River.

When he arrived, he learned that the students were not being fed even though it was a boarding school. So Raymond started a rally with the students to fight against the school. When the superintendent arrived to help deal with the situation, they called Raymond to the principal's office because he was the one leading the rally. When the superintendent began criticizing Raymond for what he was doing, Raymond hit the superintendent in the face.

Raymond was thrown out of the school and returned to Daru, where he then began dealing with drugs with his brother. He also convinced Nasa back in Kotale Village to deal drugs, too, and that is why he was called Nasty. Raymond's next plan was to take a boat to Australia where he would trade his drugs for guns from the aboriginal Australians. Then he took the guns back to PNG and crossed the Western Province border into Indonesia, where he sold them to the rebels.

Several times Raymond was arrested in PNG for selling drugs, for stealing, and for murder. At one point, he was able to escape from the prison any time he wanted, enter the town, and then return to the prison without the government knowing he had done so. Whenever you are put into prison in PNG, you are asked what religious group you belong to. Because Raymond did not understand why Christians would go to church on Sunday, he always signed his paper as a Seventh-day Adventist even though he was not one.

By 1996, Raymond had been in prison dozens of times. That is when he began to notice that almost every one of his friends had passed away because of their crimes. Raymond then decided after his final imprisonment, he would return to Kotale Village and retire from crime. He arrived back in Kotale Village at just about the time we had moved to Balimo.

Because Raymond had traveled all over PNG and into Australia, he had become proficient in English. Because he was the best English speaker in Kotale Village, I asked whether he would be willing to help him me with my project. I did not know his history at the time, but Raymond agreed and started attending our church every Sabbath. What was interesting is that when our family would fly to Port Moresby for supplies, upon our return that we would see that there were more people coming to the church every Sabbath. It was all because of Raymond.

I would hold a morning worship service every Sabbath at 6:00, then start Sabbath School at 9:30, with church service at 11:00. Then I started having Bible studies every Sabbath afternoon around 2:00. Every time I spoke, Raymond would interpret for me, English into Gogodala. Raymond asked if he could read my Ellen G. White books. We had the entire *Conflict of the Ages* Series with us there. After going through all twenty-six Bible studies, I then asked my congregation who wanted to be baptized. I was shocked when every church member raised their hand, especially, Raymond, Nasa, and Gamani.

I then made a trip to the union conference office and met with the ministerial director. I asked whether he would be willing to come to Kotale Village and baptize our church members. He agreed and we set up a schedule for the baptism. When I returned to Kotale Village, I began working on the steps that took us up to the main floor of our house. I had installed some temporary steps and as I started working to finish them, I set my machete on the top step. Then, all of a sudden, the machete dropped off the top step and landed on my ankle. The machete stabbed my ankle and actually just stood upright, without falling out. I lifted it out of my ankle and went inside to get some medicine to help fix the cut.

For several weeks I tried to get it to heal, but it kept getting worse. I did not want to travel to have someone work on my ankle because I did not want to leave before our church's first baptism was done. Then one day, I realized that if I did not go find a doctor for treatment, I might lose my entire leg. So I called Les Anderson at Adventist Aviation and had him come get us and take us up to Goroka so I could find a doctor to solve my problem.

Fortunately, I did find a good local doctor in Goroka, who gave me some injections that fixed my leg almost immediately. But then, something else happened that kept me from being able to return to Kotale Village. Les, who was the pilot, woke up the morning we were going to fly home with pain in one of his knees that was so bad he would not be able to fly. Two days later, a second pilot returned from Oceania, but his license had just expired and he had to reregister before he could fly again, so he could not fly us back, either.

For one whole week we stayed with Les Anderson and his wife because no one was able to fly us back to Kotale Village so we could prepare for our baptism ceremony. Then Thursday morning, just two days before the scheduled baptism, Les came out of his bedroom and told me that his knee had just healed, and we could fly home that day. We arrived in Kotale Village and then I took our dinghy with the outboard motor to Balimo to buy some fuel so the Balimo church members could travel to Kotale Village for the baptism ceremony and

I could go to the airport to pick up the ministerial director who was coming to baptize our church members. However, there was no two-stroke gasoline available in Balimo. All the outboard engines were two stroke brands, so that is what most people purchased.

Then as I was talking to Roy Biyama, who was the person who sold the gasoline, he came up with an idea. He told me that he did have one fifty-five-gallon tank of normal gasoline and some engineered fuel oil. So that solved the problem of our getting all the Balimo church members to Kotale Village for the Sabbath baptism celebration.

The next day, I took my dinghy up to the airport in another village to pick up the ministerial director and the Western Conference president, who both had come for the baptism ceremony. As the ministerial director got on my boat, he mentioned that he had just received a fifteen-hundred-dollar check for a mission project from someone in Australia.

That was when I told him that I had three young men who wanted to be evangelists with me and if he wanted to, he could use that check to pay those men to work with me so they could buy food instead of working in their gardens. Those three men were Raymond, Nasa, and Foxy.

The ministerial director agreed that that would be a perfect project for that donation.

That Sabbath day, forty-nine Gogodala men and women were baptized into our Kotale Village Seventh-day Adventist Church.

I needed a dugout canoe so I could travel to more places than I could with my dinghy, so I tried to get one built. But I was not able to find anyone who could. One time I traveled to a village where I was told that a man did build them to sell, but when I arrived, because I was an Adventist, I was told to leave their village immediately, and he would not build me a canoe.

The tree Wolfy donated to create our dugout canoe

Because we were going to have our last meeting with the ministerial director on Sunday morning, I asked if he would ask our church if they would build me a dugout canoe so I could spread God's word among other Gogodala Villages up and down the Aramia River. He said he would, and after he asked the question, Wolfy immediately donated a tree from his farmland and that canoe was built quicker than any canoe had ever been built. After it was finished, our church met with me at our lake where the canoe was, and we had a dedication for the canoe, that God would use it for our mission project. Then, for the next year, those three men and I traveled to five villages to study with around fifty people about the truth in the Bible.

The Gogodala people actually have a song[1] that talks about that. It is called "Wawa God." Wawa is Gogodala for *father*.

What the song means is:

Father God,

You be at the front of our own canoe.

You alone,

You hold the paddle for us.

Our family traveling in our dugout canoe

---

[1] If you want to listen to that song, login to www.teachservices.com and type in JEFF BISHOP in the SEARCH FOR A PRODUCT window and click ENTER. Then click on the book *I Saw God's Hand in Papua New Guinea*. When it opens, click on the YouTube trailer to listen to the song and see the video called *The People Between*, which AFM created for the Gogodala and Dowa mission projects in PNG.

CHAPTER 17

NEW HOUSE

About a month before we moved to Kotale Village and into the bush house that Tomas had built for us, I learned that Roy Biyama had decided to purchase a walkabout sawmill. A walkabout sawmill is a device that can be carried anywhere in the woods and used to cut down trees into whatever size and shape of wood is wanted. Roy was planning to use it to create 2x4s and smooth natural spruce wall panels.

As I was talking with Roy one day, I asked him when his walkabout sawmill was going to arrive. It was the first one ever purchased among the Gogodala people. Roy was buying it from a company in Australia, so they had to ship it to PNG before he could have it delivered to Balimo on his Cargo ship. He told me that it was supposed to arrive in December, which was when we were about to leave Balimo and move to Kotale

Village. Then he said to me, "And you will be the first person to get the first wood from that machine." That was a decision Roy had made because I had not ever asked him for wood. As soon as it arrived, Roy sent six of his employees into the woods north of Kotale Village, where Wolfy told Roy he could use his trees to get any lumber we needed to build our new main house. Roy never charged me one cent for what all his employees did, or even for the gas he used to run his walkabout sawmill.

The men immediately began cutting down trees and sawing the wood we needed to build our new main house. As I was talking to Raymond and Daniel Sewanene about our house, they told me what size they needed us to build. Then the next day when we met, I learned that they had increased the size of the house. Then a third time, they again increased the size of the house. I eventually told Daniel that we did not need a house that big, but Daniel said, "Yes, we have to build your house that size." Daniel later explained to me that if they did not create a big enough house for our family, they would be criticized by the village for not taking care of their missionaries.

So, I agreed, and we began building our house. I had been told by a former PNG missionary that when I needed to hire men to work for me, I would be able to get a dozen men to work for me for around five dollars a day. As the men who agreed to help me build our main house met with me, I asked them how much they would need for their work. Their response was that they did not want any money. What they wanted was to work for a "rice contract."

Rachel and I starting our new house

A rice contract meant that the men would arrive around seven o'clock in the morning and work until around one o'clock; then we would cook some rice for them and put some tin fish on the rice. Tin fish was fish that were packaged in metal cans that could be purchased from Roy Biyama. So every day they would work, then eat fish and rice along with hot chocolate. I would sit down on the living room floor in our bush house with the men and eat that food with them. What surprised me was that I eventually liked the fish and rice lunch we would eat every day.

Our house getting built by the men working for the "Rice Contract"

As we were building our house, the members of the ECP church were complaining. One morning, an old man arrived as Raymond and I were setting the posts and forms for the base of the house. Raymond was up on the forms when the man arrived and started yelling at Raymond for helping me. Raymond walked toward the end of the forms and attempted to jump down to fight with the man, but I stood between the two of them and told Raymond to stay up on the forms. The man then left our property.

We got it built pretty quickly, thanks to Jack Mulaki's donation of that property to our Seventh-day Adventist church. But shortly after it was done, Jack Mulaki's cousin Bob Daniya stopped at our house and knocked on our door. He did not become a pastor; instead he became a doctor, and was in charge of the children's medical department for the government of PNG. As I answered the door, Dr. Daniya told me that I had to leave the Gogodala community, and if I would not leave, then he would burn my house down. After Dr. Daniya walked off, I went to the village to contact the village chief to let him know what had just happened. The chief told me that he would organize a village meeting and would deal with the issue.

The next day, I learned that Dr. Daniya had met with the ten deacons of the Kotale Village ECP church to tell them they needed to arrange for a meeting with all of them against me; I could have only one person to serve as interpreter. The purpose of the meeting was to throw our family out of the Gogodala community.

> *The purpose of the meeting was to throw our family out of the Gogodala community.*

Then someone came and told me something that had just happened. He told me that as Dr. Daniya was discussing his plan with the deacons, one of them stood up and said, "I cannot fight against that guy, he is too strong." Then another deacon stood up and said the same thing. Within just a few minutes, every deacon agreed and said that there was no way that all ten of them, including Dr. Daniya, could fight against me. So Dr. Daniya changed his plan and told me that we would have a meeting in Balimo instead of Kotale Village, because the Kotale Village deacons could not fight against me.

The village chief told Dr. Daniya that there was no way for me to attend a meeting in Balimo, but he would have one there in Kotale Village the following morning. In the morning, the entire village arrived in front of our new house, waiting for Dr. Daniya to arrive for the meeting about removing our family. The problem was that Dr. Daniya did not arrive. Finally, the village chief sent someone down the path to tell Dr. Daniya to hurry up and get to the meeting.

When he finally showed up, the chief started talking to Dr. Daniya privately for about twenty minutes; then the two walked over to where I was standing with the village members, and Dr. Daniya poked me in my chest and said, "You have to leave this village!" Immediately three men attacked Dr. Daniya. It did not turn into an actual fight, but it did convince Dr. Daniya to leave Kotale Village. He never returned.

But a little while later, while I was traveling somewhere in PNG, Bobbi and Rachel were still at our house when they saw quite a few people out in our yard talking to each other. My wife and daughter did not know what those people were doing out in our yard, and also did not know whether they should go out to meet them or stay inside. Because the people seemed very upset, they decided to stay in the house. The people were out in our yard for thirty to forty-five minutes, and then for some reason, they all just left.

When I arrived back home, someone informed me that a very large group of people had walked to our property to burn our house down. But as they were there, they had all been asking each other who had the matches, but no one did, so they finally decided to leave. That is when Bobbi and Rachel learned what they had been facing although they didn't know at that time what actually was happening. God saved my family.

Our house finally done, even with a water tank

Our house in front of the lake

Our new school and the students that began attending our church school

CHAPTER 18

SCHOOL

Independence Day is a public holiday in Papua New Guinea, observed on September 16th. It was on September 16th in 1975 that Papua New Guinea gained its independence from Australia.

Just like July 4th in America, the entire country of PNG celebrates their day of independence. Among the Gogodala people, one of the main events is a Gogodala canoe festival. These canoes are large, magnificently carved and painted racing boats. Up to fifty men would paddle in each canoe while racing. The Gogodala had been having canoe races since the 1900s. The other thing the Gogodala have on Independence Day is dancing. When they dance, they sing songs that were created back in the old days when their community was completely made up of animists. Every school student was taught how to dance and learn to sing the old Gogodala songs, which were definitely Satanic in nature.

One afternoon, Raymond and his wife, Aina, were sitting on our living room floor with their five-year-old, son having a discussion with me, when Raymond told me that he was not happy that his son, who was in kindergarten, was having to learn the Satanic songs and dance at school for the Independence Day celebration. Then he asked if we could start a church school. Because I had been a teacher at Grand Rapids Junior Academy, I agreed with Raymond and said that if our church was willing to support that idea, then I would, too.

Raymond, who started the school

The next Sabbath it was brought up at our church, and all agreed to start a church school for their kids in Kotale Village. Not only did they agree to start a church school, they also agreed on who should run it. One of the church members who lived in Kewa Village, just down the Aramia River from Kotale Village, was already a principal at the public-school there; said that she was getting ready to retire from the government and that she would run the school.

The church became excited and the new school was started immediately. A few weeks later, the president of AFM, Clyde Morgan, had decided to take his board chairman Paul Stokstad on a trip to see a few mission projects, and one of them he wanted to see was the Gogodala project.

When they arrived, the Kotale Village people held a great celebration ceremony. Paul and his wife, Shelly, had a great time and even said it was the best visit they had ever had. Then the chairman asked me what we were building on our church's property. I told him it was the church school that Raymond had asked for. Paul then asked if we needed anything for the school. I told him that the one thing we did need was books— books for the teachers and books for the students. He asked me how much that would cost and then donated the entire amount that was needed to pay for the teachers' and the kids' books.

A few months later, the school was ready to open. One day, Raymond and I had traveled to Balimo in my new dugout canoe, and on the way back to Kotale Village just before we turned off the Aramia River and on to the creek to Kotale Village, we saw the teacher who said she would run the school. She was fishing on the Aramia River. We stopped to inform her that the school was going to be ready to open in just three days. She responded by saying that she no longer could serve as a teacher for our school.

That upset Raymond and me very much. We had completely created our church school, and even received a thousand-dollar donation for the books, and then had no one to run it. I wondered, what were we going to do? Then as we arrived back at Kotale Village, Raymond told me that he would be a teacher and run the school. Raymond then contacted another friend from Kotale Village, who agreed to help him teach the other classroom. Our school turned out to be amazing, and the students from that church school tested higher in government tests than the students in any other school among the Gogodala people. Raymond again was a great assistant for our mission project.

School children

CHAPTER 19

ANGEL

Our family needed to write an article for the AFM magazine every month and then forward it to the office in Berrien Springs, Michigan. In order to do that, we needed to have an email system in our remote village. What was amazing is that just before we left America, we were able to find a satellite phone system that we could use to call a phone number in America to do emails with.

Our satellite phone looked like a laptop computer. We would lift up the lid and face it toward the satellite position in the sky. Then we would make a phone call to connect to an email system in the United States. We were able to send email messages and also could receive emails from friends and from AFM members who needed some information.

Unfortunately, the cost to use that satellite phone was about three dollars per minute, so we would try to connect as quickly as we could, and then send and receive the emails as fast as we could. The way I set up our system was, I built a ladder outside on the back of our house about ten feet high. Then I installed a flat shelf next to the outside wall of our house where we would set the phone to connect to the satellite. I drilled a hole in the wall of our house where we would insert the wire to connect the phone to the computer in the back room of our house. I also put a round piece of wood on the outside of the wall to keep the hole protected; we would then spin it to open the hole to put the wire through.

One day, Rachel said she would go out and hook up the phone and insert the wire so I could do the email myself right away. While Bobbi and I were in the back room waiting for Rachel to connect the phone to the computer, we both kept saying, "Why is it taking so long for Rachel to connect with us?" Maybe she had not spun the round piece of wood to open the hole for inserting the wire.

After several minutes, Rachel walked into the back room, where we were waiting for her. I turned around and asked why it was taking her so long to set up the phone. Rachel responded by telling me that the strap at the top of the ladder that we used to free both hands to set up the phone had snapped, and she had just fallen straight backwards off the ladder.

The 3,000-gallon water tank for collecting rain from the roof was back there, and I had planned to put a second tank there, too; I had already installed the sixteen posts. And four of those posts were just about two feet apart, and directly in the center of that ladder where she was falling down from. Then she told us that as she was falling, someone reached out and grabbed her, and moved her sideways, between the two lines of posts, and safely laid her on the ground. Rachel couldn't see who had grabbed her, so it had to have been an angel. God definitely saved her life that day.

There was one other way God made something happen because of our computer. Our church members loved singing Christian songs. There were many songs we would sing every Sabbath. Two years after we arrived in PNG, I decided to try to

Then she told us that as she was falling, someone reached out and grabbed her, and moved her sideways, between the two lines of posts, and safely laid her on the ground.

create a Gogodala hymnal for our church. The congregation shared with me ninety-one songs they wanted me to include in the hymnal. Then they shared with me the Gogodala words for all the songs. There were two hymns that they would sing in both English and Gogodala. We also used English to sing the tune for several songs. Here are two examples we used: "Are You Washed in the Blood?" and "Blessed Assurance."

Rachel standing on my ladder with our satellite phone where she fell from and an angel saved her life

I wrote all of the songs on my computer and then copied them onto a flash drive. I decided to fly to the PNG union conference Office to see if they would be able to print copies of the hymnal for us. When I arrived, I walked into the printing department and talked to a young man from PNG who did the printing, and asked if it would be possible to print a Gogodala hymnal. Unfortunately, he told me that for some reason, they were not allowed to work overtime at all and would not be able to print a hymnal for me. He did say that sometime in the future they might be able to, so I told him thanks and gave him my flash drive.

The union conference had some apartments where people who traveled there could spend the night, so that's where we stayed until the following morning, when we were already scheduled to leave. When I got up that morning and walked outside the apartment, there was a box sitting in front of the door. I picked it up and opened it, and for some reason, that night that young man did decide to print our Gogodala hymnal. He actually wrote on the front page, "SDA Gogodala Hymnal Compiled by: Kotale SDA Church June 22, 1999."

I went back to his department and thanked him for so quickly printing our hymnal. He told me that he loved Americans and that was why he worked that night—for free—to print our hymnal.

Here is my favorite song, called "Wawa God":

Wawa God e sa:dowali gawa lopa eladele

Sa:pe keyali a: e gwalisama

Father God, You be at the front of our own canoe.

You alone, You hold the paddle for us.

(Repeat 3 times)

*Working on the computer in the back room of our house, waiting
for Rachel to connect the internet from the satellite phone*

CHAPTER 20

LOVE ONE ANOTHER

While we were living in Balimo, our only way to travel to Roy's city store was to walk. There were only two vehicles in the entire city, even though it was the Middle Fly District government center.

I would have to walk almost half a mile just to go see Roy for anything I needed. Roy then sold me a bicycle that I could ride, to make my traveling much easier. About the same time, a young boy who was in the seventh grade in Balimo's elementary school had become friends with me. He would come see me so I could help him with his homework, especially his mathematics. He would visit me almost every afternoon. He even started telling his friends that when our family would return to America, he was going to go with us as our child.

One thing he also liked about visiting me was that I would let him ride my bicycle around Balimo. There were days when people would see the child riding my bicycle and at the same time see me walking down the street in the middle of the village. That actually aggravated the people in Balimo. They wondered how that kid could take my bicycle and ride it at the same time that I had to walk down the street so, they developed a plan to stop that from happening.

What I learned later was that the men who hated that this was taking place had decided to stop the boy from riding the bicycle. What is interesting is that when they saw him one day riding my bicycle, their plan to stop him was to destroy the bicycle so he could no longer steal it from me. So to solve the problem in that manner, would also destroy my possibility of riding the bicycle, as well. But that was typical of the kind of solution the Gogodala people would choose, to solve a problem.

A similar story about solving a problem occurred in Kotale Village after we moved there. There was a woman named Dedeya. Dedeya and her husband had both joined our Adventist church in Kotale Village. One day, Dedeya told Bobbi that someone had come by her house and had stolen one of her chickens. Her husband had built a coop for her to keep her chickens in, and that was where it had been stolen from.

People were stealing things all the time. Our family would constantly have young kids stop at our home and ask if we wanted to buy some vegetables or fruits from their gardens. I always bought a lot of bananas that way. However, we were encouraged eventually to stop buying produce from those kids because they were actually stealing it from other people in the village.

It wasn't always fruit or chickens that people stole—some would also steal gasoline from individuals who had an outboard motor for their dugout canoe. I would always purchase fifty-five-gallon barrels of gas from Roy and leave them under our house. We did have lids on the tanks, but if someone had a way to remove the lid, they could steal some of my gas. One day, one of the neighbors told Bobbi that I needed to lock up my fuel drums to stop thieves from stealing it at night. But a while after, he actually said, "Well, no one is going to steal your fuel; all the thieves are now attending your church."

So because Dedeya wanted to stop people from stealing her chickens, she killed all of the chickens and destroyed the coop. It was very interesting to observe the way people would make decisions to solve problems in PNG. Police officers would also do such things in villages that they went to. They would arrive in a village and discipline people by beating people up, and sometimes actually burning down their houses to condemn the people for the crimes they had been accused of.

We actually had a clothesline system in our backyard, where we would dry our clothes. One day, a man walked into our backyard and stole one of my shirts. It was a shirt with a picture on it, that everyone in the village knew belonged to me. When that man began wearing my shirt, the people knew he had stolen it from me, so they beat him up and forced him to return it to me. Among the Gogodala, the response to people who did bad things was always to treat them very badly.

But a while after, he actually said, "Well, no one is going to steal your fuel; all the thieves are now attending your church."

As we lived among the Gogodala people, we began sharing with them other ways to treat people who were sinning and showing them that God tells us that we need to love others. We also had been sharing with them how God would forgive people for committing sins, trying to teach them not to treat people as they had been.

Whenever our family would travel to another part of PNG or even to Australia, and then return to Kotale Village, the whole village would meet us as we arrived. But one time, when we arrived, only two people met us, Foxy and one other man. The reason no one met us was that while we were gone on that trip, some kids had eaten our daughter Rachel's cat, and some wanted to hurt those kids. But Foxy told them to stop their violent punishment. At that time, the attitude was starting to change with regard to how to treat people who had committed sins.

Then one week, a man named Dodomela had been criticized by some village members for some reason, so he decided to attack the ECP church. He took a hammer and destroyed the entrance door to their church. When our church members learned that Dodomela had destroyed the ECP church door, we held a church meeting to decide what to do about his action.

I led the meeting and explained to the members that in cases where the offense is not so serious as to warrant the extreme course of removing a member, the church may express its disapproval by a vote of censure. I then asked if they wanted to censure Dodomela for one month or a little longer. However, after I asked the members what they would like to do, Nasa stood up and suggested that the church members fix the ECP church's door and help Dodomela ask them for forgiveness.

He even suggested that the church members donate the funds to repair Dodomela's damage to the ECP Church. I was very surprised that they did not follow my recommendation. What actually was taking place was, what I had been teaching the Gogodala church members about how to treat others was actually being put into practice. The Gogodala response to people's damaging or destroying things was finally beginning to change. They began to help others turn from their evil and seek God.

But then one year later, Tomas and Wolfy were no longer friends. Those were the first two men who raised their hands telling Jack Mulaki that they would keep the Sabbath. They were the two who asked if our family would move to Kotale Village. Tomas had become our head deacon and Wolfy had become our head elder. The end of their friendship came about because in our village, people never knew what time it was because no one had a clock. So when our church service would be ready to start on the Sabbath or our prayer meeting on Wednesday evenings, Tomas would arrive and bang the propane tank with a lead pipe as if it were a gong, to let the church people know it was time to arrive.

Then one Sabbath morning Tomas did not show up, so after about twenty minutes, Wolfy banged the propane tank. After our church members arrived, Tomas did, too, and was very upset that Wolfy did his job, so he would no longer shake his hand or talk to him. Because our church members would shake one another's hands every Sabbath, that proved that they no longer were friends.

What actually was taking place was, what I had been teaching the Gogodala church members about how to treat others was actually being put into practice.

The following Sabbath, they still would not talk or shake hands, so that week I decided to have a private discussion with them at one of our church member's houses. After we met, they did agree to forgive each other and become friends again. I asked them if they would be willing to meet each other in front of our members at the next church meeting right before I preached my sermon, and shake each other's hands. That would prove to our church that they loved each other again. They agreed that they would.

After our church started that next Sabbath, and after we finished our lesson study and were ready to start our church service, I walked out and knelt down as I entered the platform. After I prayed, I sat down while we had our opening song, our offering, and our children's story. While other men were doing all of that and I was sitting there in front of our church members. something entered my mind. I felt a prompting, a feeling that I needed to forgive that lady who refused to be our schoolteacher just three days before it was ready to start.

Tomas banging the propane tank with a lead pipe like it was a gong

Wolfy, who banged the propane tank because Tomas did not show up

My response was, no I can't do that right now. Then it entered my mind again. Finally, after the third time I thought about it, I decided, yes, I should do that. After we were ready for me to invite Tomas and Wolfy up to shake hands, I began by telling the lady that I was sorry I was upset that she could not become our teacher and asked her to forgive me for being upset. I then walked over to where she was sitting and hugged her and told her I loved her.

Then Tomas and Wolfy came up and demonstrated their connection to each other, too. Then about five other church members also came up and did the same thing. Our church was really becoming like God says we needed to be, loving one another.

The greenhouse where I started growing the new trees and vanilla beans

CHAPTER 21

VANILLA

If you are a citizen of PNG, you are most likely a chewer of betel nut, known locally as *buai*. Close to half of all citizens in PNG chew betel nut. It is common even for children as young as six to chew it. When they chew betel nut, their teeth become red. That is why if you see someone who does not have red teeth, then you can expect that they are probably a Seventh-day Adventist.

One day, I talked to Les Anderson, the pilot from Adventist Aviation, about the Western Highlands Mission office, in

Mt. Hagen, Papua New Guinea, where a meeting was scheduled for all the pastors and missionaries in our Adventist district. Les told me that he had an idea to share with our Adventist Church members so they might be able to raise more money. It was vanilla beans.

He told me that he had just received six vanilla cuttings that he wanted to share with church members. I asked if I could get one and he said yes, he would give me one when he came to pick me up to attend the conference. When the Adventist Aviation plane arrived to pick me up, it was not Les, it was the other pilot, so I did not get a vanilla cutting. After arriving in Mt. Hagen for the conference, we met in the church the following morning. During our first meeting, one of the pastors brought up a question. He told the pastors that one of his church members had gone into the woods in their village and climbed up a palm tree to get betel nut to take to Port Moresby, to make money.

Because betel nut is like tobacco, Seventh-day Adventists do not chew it. That pastor felt that his church members should not go out and harvest it to sell to others either. Then he asked what we should do. I raised my hand and suggested that we find some cash crop our church could recommend for its members so they could earn more money that way. Then I said, "Like vanilla beans."

The pastor talked for a couple of minutes about that option and then moved on to other matters. As I left the church after the meeting was over, a young man named Obed shook my hand and asked if I were interested in vanilla. I told him that yes, I was interested, so Obed told me to come to his house to learn about vanilla beans. Obed was there in Hagen at the conference district because he was learning how to become a pastor.

Vanilla beans growing in the greenhouse

Then what I learned was, before Obed moved there to learn how to become a pastor, he had started a vanilla bean farm that his uncle Silas Yamasombi had then taken over. When we arrived at his house, Obed showed me some vanilla beans, and told me that if I wanted to start a vanilla bean project with the Gogodala people, his uncle Silas would give me one hundred cuttings. Obed then taught me more about vanilla beans, including what trees we needed to plant in order to grow vanilla beans. Then he wrote a letter to his uncle explaining who I was and that he wanted him to give me one hundred cuttings. I put the letter in my suitcase and thanked Obed.

There was a particular tree that helped the vanilla grow better and also could be planted very easily. All you had to do was cut a branch off an existing tree and then stick it in the ground and a tree would immediately grow. Obed asked me if our village had that type of tree, but it did not. Then, on the last day of the conference meeting, one of the men went out and started cutting several branches for me to take back to my village.

What we were creating so we could grow vanilla beans to give people vanilla cuttings to start vanilla farms

Several other pastors and I were standing at the airport when the pilot arrived; this time it was Les Anderson. We all had many materials we wanted to take home, so we had way more with us now than when we were brought to Mt. Hagen originally. When Les arrived, he got out of the plane and walked over to meet, us, and he informed us that there was no way we could load all that stuff on his plane. It would be way to heavy. He even asked if I wanted the trees they had given to me, or my suitcase to fly home with. He couldn't let me take both on his airplane. I told him that I wanted the trees, not my suitcase, so I gave my suitcase to Obed and got on the plane with my tree branches.

As soon as I got back home, I told Bobbi what had happened, and that I would be heading to Wewak the very next day to see Obed's uncle to get some vanilla cuttings. When I arrived in Wewak, I asked someone if they would drive me to the Seventh-day Adventist conference department and they agreed to do that for me. When I got there and entered the office, and the president was not there but the finance director was. As I entered the room, I introduced myself and learned that the finance director already knew me. I found out that he was the one I had talked to over our ham radio a few times when he was working at the Mt. Hagen conference office. We had never met personally, but we had talked on the ham radio together. That is when I told him why I was there, and he, too, was interested in vanilla bean projects.

The next day the president arrived, and I learned that he knew me, too. He had been working for the PNG Union mission office when our family had attended the ladies' conference in Daru the year before. I told him that I was there to meet Obed's uncle to get some vanilla cuttings. The president told me that I had to meet another man named Tony instead. I didn't actually agree with him, but I did not say I wouldn't do that.

The following day, the president told me again that I had to meet that guy, Tony. The same thing happened. I didn't actually agree, but I did not say I wouldn't do as he suggested, either. Then the third time the president recommended I meet Tony, I finally said, "Okay, I will do that." The Wewak village was right on the Pacific Ocean, in East Sepik Province. Obed's uncle Silas lived in Baimuru Village, in the Yangoru District, on a road headed south toward the Sepik River. I then learned that Tony was on the same road as Silas, but three hours farther.

I heard that there was an Adventist who drove a flatbed truck that he had modified to transport people to the Sepik River. He said he would take me with him to meet Tony the following day.

For some reason, we did not leave until around nine o'clock that evening. When we finally arrived at the village where Tony, the vanilla farmer, lived, it was around two o'clock in the morning. The driver got out of his car and walked to the house of the lay pastor who served at a Seventh-day Adventist Church there, and knocked on his door. The young man got up and came out to see what the driver needed. The driver told the young man he had a visitor there to see him. What he did not tell him was that it was me, an American missionary, because he wanted to see his surprise when he met me. I was introduced to the young man and was invited into his house to sleep.

Vanilla beans growing

The following morning, the lay pastor told me that on Friday night they had vespers, and he wanted me to speak at his church. I agreed. Then around ten o'clock, the lay pastor found Tony and told him that I was the missionary who was there to see him. I then learned that Tony was his head Elder. After he met me, he took me out into his vanilla farm to show me what it was like. His farm was huge; anyone could easily get lost walking in it. He then asked me how many vanilla cuttings I would like, and I told him that I had only enough land to have a total of six hundred plants and was already getting one hundred from Obed's uncle. So Tony immediately told his workers to plan on preparing five hundred vanilla cuttings on Sunday morning for me. Then I asked Tony how much he needed me to pay for the cuttings. Usually they sold for five kina apiece.

Tony then looked at me and said, "I will not charge you anything for them. You can have them for free." That night I preached at their church, and on Sabbath the lay pastor told me that he wanted me to preach for the church service, too. Once I got to the church, the lay pastor told me that he wanted me to do the mission story for Sabbath School, too. Adventists in PNG also have a Sabbath afternoon service program called Adventist Youth (AY), and he told me that he needed me to speak at that event, as well.

Tony, who gave me 6,000 vanilla cuttings to start the vanilla project

On Sunday morning Tony gave me the five hundred cuttings and thanked me for starting a vanilla project for the Gogodala people. Then I headed back toward Obed's uncle's village and met him, and his wife, Grace. They gave me one hundred more cuttings. When I arrived back in Kotale Village, I began building a harvest facility to create vanilla cuttings to share with the Gogodala people. I actually traveled to Tony's farm three times while starting the vanilla project, and Tony ended up giving me six thousand cuttings for my Gogodala vanilla project, all free.

Kadu was the church member who helped me teach our village members how to create a vanilla farm. He would calculate the number of hours each person worked for us so we then would give them vanilla cuttings based on how many hours they worked. More than a hundred people helped us create the farm and everything we made for the vanilla project.

Because of something that had happened (I will explain later), I had to travel out of PNG to spend a month in Australia. While I was gone, two men from Europe arrived in Balimo to see how they could assist the Gogodala people in learning more about farming. While at a meeting in Balimo, one of the men asked the government officials who they needed to see to learn about the vanilla project they had heard was started in Kotale Village. I don't know how they even knew anything about our vanilla project. Just as the question was asked, Kadu was walking down the street in Balimo. One of the government officials pointed to Kadu and said, you need to ask him. He is one of the men who works with the missionary on the vanilla project.

They called Kadu into the meeting and said, "We would like to come see your vanilla farm tomorrow, is that okay?" Kadu replied, sorry, tomorrow is the Sabbath; we cannot do that, but you can come on Sunday. The men agreed to go on Sunday to see the Kotale Village vanilla project. When they arrived, Kadu showed them the farm area, the cutting facility, and the new trees that were being planted to help raise the vanilla beans.

The men asked Kadu who created the farm. He told them that their missionary did. Then they asked who planted the new trees. Again his response was, our missionary. Every question they asked about who was responsible for some aspect of the vanilla project, Kadu responded, it is our missionary. Then they asked one last question, "What did the government do to help?" Kadu responded, "They did not do anything." One of the men then put his arm around Kadu's shoulder and said, "We are going to support this vanilla project."

We created a water device to grow the vanilla cuttings more quickly

When I arrived back in Kotale Village, Kadu told me what had happened, but no donation had been delivered yet. I then took Kadu and one of our other church members, along with two of Dale Goodson's church members, back to Obed's uncle's farm, where he taught them all how to grow vanilla beans; at that point I had to get ready to move back to America. An interesting thing about growing vanilla beans is that every morning you have to go out to your vanilla plants to see if any flowers have appeared. When they finally do bloom, the flowers only stay open for one day and have to be carefully pollinated within twelve hours.

Pollination is the act of transferring pollen grains from the male anther of a flower to the female stigma. The other thing is that you personally are the only one who can pollinate the vanilla flowers on every orchid. You have to hand pollinate every flower yourself. That was the most complicated issue that Silas taught us. Obed's uncle Silas did a great job.

Ten years later, when I traveled back to Kotale Village, I learned that Jack Mulaki was the man the government hired to run the vanilla project. When I arrived, I met with Jack, who was the one who originally donated his property for our church, and he told me an amazing thing. He told me that the Europeans who had met with Kadu did donate some money. They actually donated two hundred thousand dollars for the Gogodala vanilla project. Jack also told me that all of Western Province was then growing vanilla beans, and every farmer who was growing them knew my name. They had already sold six tons of vanilla beans.

Obed's uncle Silas Yamasombi teaching us how to pollinate the vanilla flowers

The last amazing thing Jack Mulaki shared with me was that his cousin, Bob Daniya, who was the one who had wanted to burn down our house, was then the governor of Western Province. Because of the vanilla project in that province, he was then telling people to listen to what the Adventists were telling them.

Kadu pollinating the vanilla flower

CHAPTER 22

ILLNESS

I n 1998, Stacy had finished her junior and senior years of home school with us there in Kotale Village, and was headed back to America to attend college. Because we had our satellite phone, we would call her in America once a month and talk to her for only about ten minutes. Then one day in 2001, I learned that Stacy had gotten engaged. A few months later, Bobbi and I traveled back to America for their wedding. Shortly after, we flew back to PNG.

When we arrived back in Port Moresby, we had to stay there for a couple of weeks for Bobbi to have some tooth surgery. Then we flew back to Balimo. After arriving in Balimo, we got in my dugout canoe and headed up the Aramia River to Kotale Village. Just as we passed Kewa Village and turned right onto the creek that took us to Kotale Village, I was happy to be almost back home. When we arrived, Bobbi entered the house and I told her that I needed to go out to check on the vanilla farm. When I got back to the house, Bobbi was crawling on her knees toward the bathroom. I asked her what was wrong, and she said she had a fever and was in a lot of pain.

She took the malaria medicine, but it did not help. The fever would not go away. The following day, Tomas and I took her to the Balimo hospital in our dugout canoe. When we arrived, we had her admitted, and I began trying to call Adventist Aviation on our satellite phone to ask Les Anderson if he could come pick us up so we could take her to Port Moresby, where there was a real hospital.

Unfortunately, Les told me that the weather was too bad for flying that day. Later that afternoon, I called Les again to see how the weather was, but when I hooked up our satellite phone to Roy's electrical outlet, I was not told that they had changed it from 110v to 220v, and it destroyed our phone. Then the only way I could then contact Adventist Aviation was to travel back to our home and use our ham radio. I told Bobbi that I was headed back to Kotale Village to contact Les and would be back the following day.

The next morning, at 6:00, a young man arrived at the hospital to see Bobbi. When he entered, he informed her that he had been studying the Bible with me, and that in the night an angel had arrived and given him two statements he was supposed to tell her. First, he told her that the angel told him that she would not die. Next, he told her that the Gogodala project *would move forward*. Then he mentioned my Gogodala name Ba:kele, which meant *rock*, and that that would be the foundation for the Gogodala project.

While Bobbi was in the hospital, the nurses injected the malaria medicine into her veins, but it was not lowering her temperature. So the nurse started wiping down her skin to try to lower her temperature, and she kept taking her temperature with a thermometer. As the day progressed, Bobbi became weaker and eventually became semi-conscious. She could

> *As she took what she thought was her last breath, all of a sudden, she remembered what that young man told her earlier that morning.*

not talk any more, but she could hear what people were saying. That's when she heard the nurse tell her best friend Malawato, who was also a nurse, that she was not going to survive, and so to prepare for death.

A little while later, Bobbi became so sick, she was having difficulty breathing. She realized that she was going to die, and she asked God to forgive her and take care of me and our daughters. As she took what she thought was her last breath, all of a sudden, she remembered what that young man told her earlier that morning. Immediately she opened her eyes and began talking to the nurse and the fever dropped. Because of what she had just witnessed, the nurse threw her thermometer and towel into the air and ran out of the room to tell Malawato, she is going to survive!

That afternoon when I arrived to tell her that Les Anderson would be coming the following day to fly us to Port Moresby, I learned what had just happened. God had saved my wife's life.

CHAPTER 23

TEACHING AGAIN

After Les Anderson was able to fly us to Port Moresby, Bobbi became a little better, but we had to move to Australia, where she could stay until she was completely recovered from her sickness. I would fly to Australia and stay with her for four weeks, then fly back to PNG to the Gogodala project for two weeks. On my third trip to PNG, I returned from Kotale Village to Port Moresby and used one of the university professor's computers to check my emails. When I pulled up my email, I saw an email from an education superintendent from the Iowa/Missouri Conference who asked if I would be willing to teach in their conference back in America.

I responded by answering all of the superintendent's questions, and then informed him that our mission project was not yet done, so I could not actually teach right then. That evening, when I called Bobbi in Australia to tell her that I was back to Port Moresby, and would be arriving in Australia the next day, I told her about the email I had just gotten from that education superintendent who had asked me if I would go there to teach.

She asked what my response was. I told her that I had replied by saying that I could not come at that time because the Gogodala project was not yet complete. Then she told me that she needed to share something with me. She told me that she had been talking to my mother the day before, and mentioned to her that she wished God would tell us what we needed to do. We did not know how to decide whether we should return to America or just stay in PNG and Australia. My mother said, "I think He has shown you that you need to come back to the America because of your illness." Bobbi then realized that she had not even asked God whether we should return to America.

After hanging up with my mother, she prayed, asking God to have someone send me a request to teach at one of their schools, without me even notifying anyone that I wanted to, so that we would know we were finally supposed to leave PNG and the Gogodala project. It was on that very same day that I had gotten that email from the Iowa/Missouri Conference asking me to come teach in their district.

The amazing thing was that the education director had asked the ministerial director who he would suggest for a teaching position in their district, and he said Jeff Bishop. He knew me because when I was teaching at Grand Rapids Junior Academy, his two sons were in my classroom. When he traveled to a mission project once for two weeks to do evangelism, his two sons stayed with us. The education director had actually asked the ministerial director's wife to send me an email asking if I would like to come teach in their district, because we already knew each other.

What I later learned was that she had written me an email three times, but because of emergency phone calls and other issues, she had to delete the emails and never sent them to me. Then one day, the education director finally walked into the office and said, "Can you just give me Jeff's email address; I will contact him myself." And the email arrived exactly the same day that Bobbi had requested that God send me an email to ask me if I would want to teach in their district if we were to move back to America. We still did not know what Bobbi's issue was, but after moving back to America we learned that she had Lyme Disease.

A year before we left, another missionary family arrived. They were living in Balimo, and worked for AFM until David and Cindy White arrived in 2004 and lived in our home in Kotale Village. Then the Ericksons arrived in 2007, and they are still working there now, in 2022, the publication date of this book. The Sligers, who arrived in 2021, are there now, too. So the messenger sent by God was correct, that my wife would not die and the project *would go forward*!

CHAPTER 24

RETURN TO GOGODALA FAMILY

Because we had to leave the Gogodala mission project in 2002, I decided to travel back to see my Gogodala friends in 2006. My uncle Chuck said he wanted to travel with me, so we left America and arrived in Port Moresby. We went to Pacific Adventist University to sleep the night before our flight to Balimo. We arrived at the airport in the morning, but not one person was there for a flight scheduled at that time. I was surprised, because there were always so many people trying to fly there in PNG. I was able to find an employee who I could ask what was going on.

Unfortunately, he told me that they found water in the gas in the airplane that morning, so our flight had been canceled. He told me just to return the next day to try to fly to Balimo. The following morning the airport was filled with people ready to fly, just like it always had been during the time I was in PNG. As my uncle and I were in line, waiting to be scheduled to fly, a man standing in front of me turned around and said, "Hi Jeff, what brought you back to PNG?" I was shocked that someone I knew was right in front of me. I told him we were flying to Balimo and he said, "You two go ahead of me."

As we arrived at the check-in counter, the person asked for our tickets. He asked how much we weighed and then told us he needed our suitcases to calculate their weight, too. Then he told me, you are the last two who can fly, so my friend saved our flight by letting my uncle and me get in front of him. We entered the waiting room, where we would wait for the airplane to arrive, and I learned that we were not actually flying to Balimo, where David White was to pick us up to take us to Kotale Village. This flight was landing up the Aramia River, in Awaba Village, at a different airport.

Kotale Village, my destination, was halfway between Balimo and that other airport, so I assumed I would have to see if someone there at that village could take us by canoe down the river to Kotale Village. When we started flying, we first landed at some village on the way to Awaba Village. Then we left and headed to another airport and landed again. At that airport, we were told we had to leave the airplane so they could fill it up with gas again.

As my uncle and I were off the airplane, I saw an Australian man walk away from the airplane, very angry. As he passed, he told me that he was thrown off the plane and had to stay in that village and fly the following day, so I walked over to talk to the pilot and ask him why that guy had to leave our airplane.

The pilot told me that because the next village we were headed to, which the Australian man was flying to, did not have any gas so he could not fly there, and that was why he had to leave. Then the pilot asked me a question. He said, "Where were you wanting to fly to?" Because I wanted to fly to Balimo, but not to Awaba Village, I told him, "I want to fly to Balimo."

He replied, "Okay, I will change our flight and we will now fly to Balimo instead of Awaba Village."

When we did arrive in Balimo, Roy Biyama's truck was there at the airport, and his employee picked us up and took us into the village, and as we were passing one building, our new Gogodala missionary, David White, saw us and was able to pick us up and transport us in his canoe with an engine to Kotale Village. In several ways, God had solved our flight problems.

Wolfy, my Gogodala father

CHAPTER 25

AFM VIDEO

In 2010, our new Gogodala missionary family, David and Cindy White, arrived in America on a furlough that all missionaries take every three years. They met us at our house, and one morning while David and I were eating breakfast, he told me that my Gogodala father, Wolfy, was no longer even able to attend church because he could no longer walk. He had been our church's head elder.

Then David told me that because he expected Wolfy was getting close to passing away, if I wanted to meet with him before he died, I should plan a visit in less than a year. I agreed that I needed to go see him and I also wanted to have a family celebration for him when I came. Because I had to build my pools during the warm season in Tennessee, I had to schedule my visit for right after Christmas that year. When I arrived in January of 2011, I purchased the food for the family celebration and met with Wolfy and his wife. He was really ill, but we did meet and talk quite a bit. I even brought them a small book I had published along with our daughters' husbands and our grandkids.

Around one hundred family members showed up at our celebration. It was a great visit. But there was a problem. Wolfy's wife was blind at that point, and she could not even see the pictures I brought for them. But at least my Gogodala father, Wolfy, was still alive.

Me and my Gogodala father, Wolfy, on my visit in 2011, three weeks before he passed away

After my visit, David asked if I wanted to travel back to Balimo on Wednesday for prayer meeting at the new church there. I told him that I did want to do that and when we arrived, they had their meeting. When they were done, they asked if I could share some information with them. When I was finished, one woman raised her hand and asked if she could share some of her information with me. I said, "Yes you can," so she started telling me something that happened to her.

Me and my Gogodala mother, Wolfy's wife, in 2011

About two years earlier, she somehow destroyed her back. She did not know what actually had happened, but she was paralyzed from the waist down. She could no longer walk. Because the government deals with people's health issues, they flew her from Balimo to Port Moresby and sent her to a hospital. A doctor examined her back, but told her he could not treat her.

He did tell her that she could take some drugs, but if she lived in America, the drugs would cost her two hundred dollars per day; she could not afford it. All she could do was lie on a bed in the hospital. It is interesting that people in that hospital would sleep in a very large room. There were beds along both outside walls and double sets of beds in the middle of the room. There were four televisions, one in each corner of the room, up near the ceiling so anyone could watch any show they had.

While she was lying on her bed, for some reason heard someone singing a Christian song in her Gogodala language. She was shocked that someone in the city was singing in her personal language. In PNG there are over 850 different languages, and most of them also have different dialects. That is why she was shocked she was hearing her language there at that hospital. The song she was hearing was "Wawa God."

Then she started looking at the television and noticed it was about the Gogodala mission project that I had started. If you watch the AFM video called *The People Between,* which she was watching, you would see that it began with the Gogodala project and then went on to the Dowa project that the Davidsons were running. But the Gogodala project was the first part. Because the Dowa people did not sing hymns when the video was created, every song on the video was from our church in Kotale Village, in her Gogodala language.

I had them sing a dozen hymns for AFM so they could share them with the donators for our project. While watching the video of *The People Between,* she told me that when she saw me walking through our village, which was at the end of the Gogodala project part of the video, she said, "Okay, God, yes I will keep the Sabbath." Immediately her back pain was gone. She sat up in her bed and then stood up and started walking in the hospital.

Then she walked back to the doctor's office and told him that God had just healed her back because she agreed to keep his Holy Day, and she needed to return to Balimo. What I also knew was that it was 3ABN who owned that television program, and it was 3ABN who had played *The People Between* video on their program that convinced her to follow God and became healed!

On my trip to the Gogodala villages in 2011, I also met with the young man in Balimo who had met with Bobbi and told her she would not die and that the Gogodala project *would move forward.* Because I was not the person he had met with to share his visit with the angel, I wanted to verify what he actually was told by that angel. So right after we met, I asked him, "So what exactly did that angel tell you about my wife?" And his response was, "No, it was not an angel, it was Jesus Christ Himself." So it was apparently Jesus Christ Himself who convinced us to start the Gogodala project and then said it *would move forward,* and it did!

> *Immediately her back pain was gone. She sat up in her bed and then stood up and started walking in the hospital.*

I also learned that my Gogodala father, Wolfy, did pass away just two weeks after I left Kotale Village and headed back to America. God did keep him alive until I was able to see him that last time. Then just a couple of months later I also learned that his wife, my Gogodala mother, could see again, so God restored her vision so she could see our families' pictures.

The day before I flew from Port Moresby to Balimo to meet with David White so he could take me to Kotale Village, he called and told me that Adventist Aviation was flying them and the Ericksons back to Port Moresby when I was leaving

Balimo, so if I wanted to fly with them, it would be cheaper and I could cancel my normal flight back to Port Moresby. I did go ahead and cancel my return. But after I arrived and met everyone, Adventist Aviation contacted David and told him he had flown too many hours, so he had to reschedule their flight for the next month. Now I was in trouble again. I went to see the flight department in Balimo, and they said they had no scheduled flights for about two more weeks.

Me and Roy Biyama, the person whose brother convinced him to close his store on Sabbath and then said I was his missionary and gave us a house and God used to solve hundreds of items our family needed to start the Gogodala mission project

I did not know what to do. Then about two days before I needed to fly back to Port Moresby, David and I met with Roy Biyama, who was then a member of parliament. While we were talking, David told him about my problem of not being able to fly back to Port Moresby. Then Roy told me something interesting. He told me that he, too, had a problem flying back to Port Moresby. He had traveled from there to Balimo for Christmas with his entire family, about eight people, and could not schedule a flight. So he had hired a pilot to pick him up. Then he said, "Jeff, you take my seat and fly back to Port Moresby." I asked him how much I needed to pay him, and he said, "No, you do not have to pay me anything, just head back home." God again made possible my visit to my favorite friends in our world!

After we left in 2002 David and Cindy White served from 2004 to 2012. Then in 2007 Stephen and Laurie Erickson arrived to serve and as of 2022, they are still serving as missionaries for the Gogodala people. They also built an "Evangelist Training Center" in Kewa village so they could teach Gogodala people to become evangelists. Then in 2020, Jason and Midori Sliger also joined the Gogodala mission project. Jason will now be working for the "Evangelist Training Center" too. The statement Jesus made that the mission project would move forward is TRUE!

The Evangelist Training Center

TEACH Services, Inc.
P U B L I S H I N G
www.TEACHServices.com ● (800) 367-1844

We invite you to view the complete
selection of titles we publish at:
www.TEACHServices.com

We encourage you to write us
with your thoughts about this,
or any other book we publish at:
info@TEACHServices.com

TEACH Services' titles may be purchased in
bulk quantities for educational, fund-raising,
business, or promotional use.
bulksales@TEACHServices.com

Finally, if you are interested in seeing
your own book in print, please contact us at:
publishing@TEACHServices.com
We are happy to review your manuscript at no charge.

CPSIA information can be obtained
at www.ICGtesting.com
Printed in the USA
JSHW031037061222
34407JS00015B/19